W9-AZU-998

Experiencing
GOD'S
Power
Today

Other Titles
by Smith Wigglesworth

Experiencing GOD'S Power Today

Smith Wigglesworth

WHITAKER
HOUSE

Whitaker House gratefully acknowledges and thanks Glenn Gohr and the entire staff of the Flower Pentecostal Heritage Center in Springfield, Missouri, and Rev. Desmond Cartwright of the Donald Gee Centre for Pentecostal and Charismatic Research in Mattersey, England, for graciously assisting us in compiling the sermons of Smith Wigglesworth for publication in this book.

Publisher's note: The messages in this book have been edited for today's reader by updating Smith Wigglesworth's words, expressions, and sentence structure. In addition, the *New King James Version* has been chosen as the principle Bible version for clarity and ease of understanding. Our singular aim has been to aid in the comprehension of Wigglesworth's unique phraseology while retaining the vital substance of his messages.

Unless otherwise noted, Scripture quotations are taken from the *New King James Version* (NKJV), © 1979, 1980, 1982, 1984 by Thomas Nelson, Inc. Used by permission. All rights reserved. Scripture quotations marked (KJV) are taken from the King James Version of the Holy Bible.

EXPERIENCING GOD'S POWER TODAY

ISBN-13: 978-0-88368-596-9 • ISBN-10: 0-88368-596-5
Printed in the United States of America
© 2000 by Whitaker House

Whitaker House
1030 Hunt Valley Circle
New Kensington, PA 15068
www.whitakerhouse.com

Library of Congress Cataloging-in-Publication Data

Wigglesworth, Smith, 1859–1947.
Experiencing God's power today
   p. cm.
ISBN 0-88368-596-5 (alk. paper)
1. Spiritual Life—Pentecostal churches. I. Title.
BV4501.2.W51918 2000
248.4'8994—dc21

00-038218

5 6 7 8 9 10 11 12 13 14 **W** 16 15 14 13 12 11 10 09

Contents

Introduction

An encounter with Smith Wigglesworth was an unforgettable experience. This seems to be the universal reaction of all who knew him or heard him speak. Smith Wigglesworth was a simple yet remarkable man who was used in an extraordinary way by our extraordinary God. He had a contagious and inspiring faith. Under his ministry, thousands of people came to salvation, committed themselves to a deeper faith in Christ, received the baptism in the Holy Spirit, and were miraculously healed. The power that brought these kinds of results was the presence of the Holy Spirit, who filled Smith Wigglesworth and used him in bringing the good news of the Gospel to people all over the world. Wigglesworth gave glory to God for everything that was accomplished through his ministry, and he wanted people to understand his work only in this context, because his sole desire was that people would see Jesus and not himself.

Smith Wigglesworth was born in England in 1859. Immediately after his conversion as a boy, he had a concern for the salvation of others and won people to Christ, including his mother. Even so, as a young man, he could not express himself well enough to give a testimony in church, much less preach a sermon. Wigglesworth said that his mother had the same difficulty in expressing herself that he did. This family trait, coupled with the fact that he had no formal education because he began working twelve hours a day at the age of seven to help support the family, contributed to Wigglesworth's awkward speaking style. He became a plumber by trade, yet he continued to devote himself to winning many people to Christ on an individual basis.

In 1882, he married Polly Featherstone, a vivacious young woman who loved God and had a gift of preaching and evangelism. It was she who taught him to read and who became his closest confidant and strongest supporter. They both had compassion for the poor and needy in their community, and they opened a mission, at which Polly preached. Significantly, people were miraculously healed when Wigglesworth prayed for them.

In 1907, Wigglesworth's circumstances changed dramatically when, at the age of forty-eight, he was baptized in the Holy Spirit. Suddenly, he had a new power that enabled him to preach, and even his wife was amazed at the transformation. This was the beginning of what became a worldwide evangelistic and healing ministry that reached thousands. He eventually ministered in the United States, Australia, South Africa, and all over Europe. His ministry extended up to the time of his death in 1947.

Several emphases in Smith Wigglesworth's life and ministry characterize him: a genuine, deep compassion for the unsaved and sick; an unflinching belief in the Word of God; a desire that Christ should increase and he should decrease (John 3:30); a belief that he was called to exhort people to enlarge their faith and trust in God; an emphasis on the baptism in the Holy Spirit with the manifestation of the gifts of the Spirit as in the early church; and a belief in complete healing for everyone of all sickness.

Smith Wigglesworth was called "The Apostle of Faith" because absolute trust in God was a constant theme of both his life and his messages. In his meetings, he would quote passages from the Word of God and lead lively singing to help build people's faith and encourage them to act on it. He emphasized belief in the fact that God could do the impossible. He had great faith in what God could do, and God did great things through him.

Wigglesworth's unorthodox methods were often questioned. As a person, Wigglesworth was reportedly courteous, kind, and gentle. However, he became forceful when dealing with the Devil, whom he believed caused all sickness. Wigglesworth said the reason he spoke bluntly and acted forcefully with people was that he knew he needed to get their attention so they could focus on God. He also had such anger toward the Devil and sickness that he acted in a seemingly rough way. When he prayed for people to be healed, he would often hit or punch them at the place of their problem or illness. Yet no one was hurt by this startling treatment. Instead, they were remarkably healed. When he was asked why he treated people in this manner, he said that he was not hitting the people but that he was hitting the Devil. He believed that Satan should never be treated gently or allowed to get away with anything. About twenty people were reportedly raised from the dead after he prayed for them. Wigglesworth himself was healed of appendicitis and kidney stones, after which his personality softened and he was more gentle with those who came to him for prayer for healing. His abrupt manner in ministering may be attributed to the fact that he was very serious about his calling and got down to business quickly.

Although Wigglesworth believed in complete healing, he encountered illnesses and deaths that were difficult to understand. These included the deaths of his wife and son, his daughter's lifelong deafness, and his own battles with kidney stones and sciatica.

He often seemed paradoxical: compassionate but forceful, blunt but gentle, a well-dressed gentleman whose speech was often ungrammatical or confusing. However, he loved God with everything he had, he was steadfastly committed to God and to His Word, and he didn't rest until he saw God move in the lives of those who needed Him.

In 1936, Smith Wigglesworth prophesied about what we now know as the charismatic movement. He accurately predicted that the established mainline denominations would experience revival and the gifts of the Spirit in a way that would surpass even the Pentecostal movement. Wigglesworth did not live to see the renewal, but as an evangelist and prophet with a remarkable healing ministry, he had a tremendous influence on both the Pentecostal and charismatic movements, and his example and influence on believers is felt to this day.

Without the power of God that was so obviously present in his life and ministry, we might not be reading transcripts of his sermons, for his spoken messages were often disjointed and ungrammatical. However, true gems of spiritual insight shine through them because of the revelation he received through the Holy Spirit. It was his life of complete devotion and belief in God and his reliance on the Holy Spirit that brought the life-changing power of God into his messages.

As you read this book, it is important to remember that Wigglesworth's works span a period of several decades, from the early 1900s to the 1940s. They were originally presented as spoken rather than written messages, and necessarily retain some of the flavor of a church service or prayer meeting. Some of the messages were Bible studies that Wigglesworth led at various conferences. At his meetings, he would often speak in tongues and give the interpretation, and these messages have been included as well. Because of Wigglesworth's unique style, the sermons and Bible studies in this book have been edited for clarity, and archaic expressions that would be unfamiliar to modern readers have been updated.

In conclusion, we hope that as you read these words of Smith Wigglesworth, you will truly sense his complete trust and unwavering faith in God and take to heart one of his favorite sayings: "Only believe!"

Faith's Laughter

"My faith pure, my joy sure."

God told Abraham, *"In Isaac* ["laughter," Hebrew] *your seed shall be called"* (Gen. 21:12). Faith is the great inheritance, for *"the just shall live by faith"* (Rom. 1:17). For twenty-five years, Abraham waited for God to fulfill His promise to give him a son. He looked to God, who never fails, and believed His Word. As we live in the Spirit, we live in the process of God's mind, and act according to His will.

Could a child be born? Yes! According to the law of faith in God who had promised. There is no limitation when you place your faith in God. *"Therefore it is of faith that it might be according to grace"* (Rom. 4:16). Grace is God's inheritance in the soul that believes.

Faith always brings a fact, and a fact brings joy. Faith! Faith! Making us know that God exists, *"and that He is a rewarder of those who diligently seek Him"*

(Heb. 11:6). *"God, who gives life to the dead and calls those things which do not exist as though they did"* (Rom. 4:17)! Those who trust God lack nothing. He gives life to the dead. The more Abraham was pressed, the more he rejoiced.

> *Not being weak in faith, he did not consider his own body, already dead (since he was about a hundred years old), and the deadness of Sarah's womb. He did not waver at the promise of God through unbelief, but was strengthened in faith, giving glory to God, and being fully convinced that what He had promised He was also able to perform.* (Rom. 4:19–21)

Abraham became *"heir of the world...through the righteousness of faith"* (v. 13). God gave life to what was dead. The more there was no hope, the more Abraham believed in hope (v. 18). If we knew the value of our trials, we would praise God for them. It is in the furnace of affliction that God gets us to the place where He can use us. Paul said concerning difficulty, "I do and will rejoice." (See Philippians 1:18.) *"For I know that this will turn out for my deliverance through your prayer and the supply of the Spirit of Jesus Christ...[that] Christ will be magnified in my body"* (vv. 19–20). Before God puts you in the furnace, He knows that you will make it through it. He never gives us anything that is above what we are able to bear. (See 1 Corinthians 10:13.)

If you know that the baptism of the Holy Spirit is taught in the Scriptures, never rest until God gives it to you. If you know that it is scriptural to be healed of every weakness—to be holy and pure, to overcome in the midst of all conditions—never rest until you are an overcomer.

If you have seen the face of God, and have had vision and revelation, never rest until you attain to it.

> *That the God of our Lord Jesus Christ, the Father of glory, may give to you the spirit of wisdom and revelation in the knowledge of Him, the eyes of your understanding being enlightened; that you may know what is the hope of His calling, what are the riches of the glory of His inheritance in the saints, and what is the exceeding greatness of His power toward us who believe.* (Eph. 1:17–19)

Holy men spoke as God gave them power and utterance. (See 2 Peter 1:21.) We must be blameless amid the crooked attitudes and behavior of the world. (See Philippians 2:15.) Jesus is the type of Sonship that we are to attain to. He was God's pattern, the *"firstfruits"* (1 Cor. 15:20), clothed with power. You must go in His name, so that when you lay hands on the sick, Satan has no power, and when you command in Jesus' name, the Enemy has to go.

> The walls are falling down,
> The walls are falling down;
> Oh, praise the Lord, praise His name,
> The walls are falling down.

Let us take God's Word and stand upon it as our strength to resist the Devil, until he is forced to flee. (See James 4:7.) Amen, amen.

The Rock Faith

Only *believe*" (Mark 5:36). Let us hear and believe the Word of God by the Spirit's power. Let us be changed by the grace of God, changed by the revelation of God. *"Only believe."* I have no other refuge than this command of Jesus.

"If you can believe" (Mark 9:23). We should be awake to the fact that we must believe; we must know the Scriptures and rest unconditionally, absolutely, upon the Word of God. God has never failed anyone who relied on His Word. Some human plan or your mind may come between you and God's Word, but rest upon what God's Word says. *"Only believe."* Oh, the charm of that truth, making you rich forever, taking away all weariness.

Those who put their trust in God are like Mount Zion; they cannot be moved (Ps. 125:1). "Rock of Ages, cleft for me." Oh, the almightiness of God's plan for us; it is tremendous. We are only weak and helpless when we forget the visitation of the Lord. From the uttermost to the uttermost. (See Mark 13:27 KJV.) *"Ask, and it will be given to you; seek, and you will find; knock, and it will be opened to you"* (Matt. 7:7).

ON THIS ROCK

When Jesus came into the region of Caesarea Philippi, He asked His disciples, saying, "Who do men say that I, the Son of Man, am?"... Simon Peter answered and said, "You are the Christ, the Son of the living God." Jesus answered and said to him, "Blessed are you, Simon Bar-Jonah, for flesh and blood has not revealed this to you, but My Father who is in heaven. And I also say to you that you are Peter, and on this rock I will build My church, and the gates of Hades shall not prevail against it. And I will give you the keys of the kingdom of heaven, and whatever you bind on earth will be bound in heaven, and whatever you loose on earth will be loosed in heaven." (Matt. 16:13, 16–19)

Jesus was full of ideals, perfect in those He was dealing with. Jesus came with a perfect purpose, so that many might hear and live and come into apostolic conditions, into divine life. Jesus was the *"firstfruits"* (1 Cor. 15:20) in order to bring to the disciples the knowledge that they were in a divine act to supersede every last power in the world. Holiness is the keynote. Saving grace is a revelation from heaven. Christ within sets up the heavenly standard, the heavenly mind, so that we live, act, and think in a new world.

Jesus asked His disciples, *"Who do men say that I, the Son of Man, am?"* (Matt. 16:13). Then Peter, with eyes and heart aflame, said, *"You are the Christ, the Son of the living God"* (v. 16). Jesus, perceiving in a moment that the revelation had come from heaven, said, *"Blessed are you, Simon Bar-Jonah, for flesh and blood has not revealed this to you, but My Father who is in heaven"* (Matt. 16:17).

God's great plan is that His children should be salt for a world that is diseased. *"You are the salt of the earth....You are the light of the world"* (Matt. 5:13–14). To be saved is to have the revelation of the glory of Christ. It is our inheritance to have the evidence of the Holy Spirit upon us. We are to be sons with power (see Romans 1:4), manifestations of the Son, built upon *"the faith of the Son of God"* (Gal. 2:20 KJV). *"On this rock I will build My church, and the gates of Hades shall not prevail against it"* (Matt. 16:18).

Interpretation of Tongues

God is visiting the earth with His resplendent glory. His coming is to revive, to heal, to deliver from the power of the pit. The ransom is the Lord, and He comes to save the oppressed, whose eyes, ears, and heart will see, hear, and feel with a new beauty.

UNCONQUERABLE FAITH

The Holy Spirit abides in power in the innermost soul, for the King has come to fill and rule the body, and to transform the life. A new creature is formed who is pure and holy, a perfect preservation and manifestation over all the powers of evil. Jesus is so sweet; He is the most lovely of all. (See Song 5:16.) *"A bruised reed He will not break, and smoking flax He will not quench"* (Isa. 42:3).

God has designed, by the Holy Spirit, to bring forth divine character in us. *"As He is, so are we in this world"* (1 John 4:17). God has saved and chosen and equipped us so that those bound by Satan may go free. Jesus was speaking to the disciples about a plan of ministry. He said, *"Most assuredly, I say to you, he who believes in Me, the works that I do he will do also; and greater works than these he will do, because I go to My Father"* (John 14:12). This truth, faith, and Christ's rock are one and the same structure: rock! *"On this rock I will build My church, and the gates of Hades shall not prevail against it"* (Matt. 16:18).

Rock! It is emblematic of a living faith, a divine principle—what God the Holy Spirit has to create and bring forth within us. No devil or evil power should be allowed to remain where we are. Jesus was teaching His disciples that, as they believed, greater things would be accomplished because He was going to the Father. *"On this rock,"* on this living faith, *"I will build My church."*

"Whatever you bind on earth will be bound in heaven, and whatever you loose on earth will be loosed in heaven" (v. 19). Keep this truth in mind, for Satan has tremendous power in the world, and people suffer as they never would if they only knew the truth, which cannot be denied. *"On this rock I will build My church"*: on this rock, this living faith, the kingdom, the new birth that has come with power (1 Thess. 1:5).

I have an awful responsibility, because unless I believe and act on this truth, it will not be operative in others. More than ninety percent of all diseases are caused by satanic power. How many here received a touch from Jesus this afternoon and were loosed from their pains? How was this accomplished? By binding and destroying the evil power in the name of Jesus. Jesus said that not only are we given power to loose and bind, but also that the gates of hell will not prevail against His church.

However, when we are ministering to others, we must know the fellowship of Christ's sufferings (Phil. 3:10). He has suffered for the people, and there also must be an entering in, a compassion, on our part. We are to be moved in union with needy sufferers. Jesus was *"moved with compassion."* (See, for example, Matthew 9:36.) Oh, the compassion of Jesus! We must be moved, the compassion taking us to the place of delivering the people.

God knows all about this meeting, and we have power to bind or loose in the name of Jesus. Who will believe? *"Have ye received the Holy Ghost since ye believed?"* (Acts 19:2 KJV). After God has saved you by His power, He wants you to be illuminators of the King, new creations. The King is already on the throne, and the Holy Spirit has come to reveal the fullness of the power of His ministry.

To be filled with the Holy Spirit is to be filled with prophetic illumination. The baptism in the Holy Spirit brings divine utterance, the divine bringing out pure prophecy. Then it becomes a state of being. God is our foundation; the Word of God is our standing. We are here to glorify God. I know how weak I am. Are we to struggle? No, no! We are to believe what God has said. We must be in our place, ready for the opportunity. God wants to give us divine life from heaven. The gates of hell will not prevail against it. The rock of deliverance comes by the key of faith. You will open the kingdom of heaven and shut the gates of hell. You will bind and loose in Jesus' name.

Interpretation of Tongues
He comes with the truth. Know His strength for the broken and the helpless. He reveals His strength. A great tide of revival spirit. Clothed

with His Spirit, the Lord will give you light. Fall down and worship Him.

Ask what you will (John 15:7). *"Whatever things you ask when you pray, believe"* (Mark 11:24). Believe! *"You will have them"* (v. 24)!

A New Epoch—
A Divine Vocation

Faith is an action, a changing. If we dare to believe God's Word, He moves and changes situations. Our purpose is to let the Holy Spirit glorify God through us. *"Only believe!"* (Mark 5:36). It will be to you as you believe (Matt. 9:29).

Hebrews 11 is called the Faith Chapter. A bundle of treasure of divine purpose, God unfolds His truth to us, and through us to others. Dare to believe God; He will not fail. Faith is the greatest subject; in it is power to lay hold of the Word of God.

It is God who brings us into victory through the blood of the slain Lamb (Rev. 12:11). Faith quickens us into a divine order, a living new source, a holy nature, having divine rights through Jesus. It is a new epoch, a new vocation; it is white hot!

As it is written: "Eye has not seen, nor ear heard, nor have entered into the heart of man the things which God has prepared for those who love Him." But God has revealed them to us through His Spirit. (1 Cor. 2:9–10)

We must be ablaze with passion for souls, so that someone may catch a new ray to bring in a new day, for the end is not yet. Praise the Lord! Glory!

Jesus Is the Author and Finisher of Our Faith

"Faith is the substance" (Heb. 11:1); it is bigger than we know. It has power to express the new creation and bring forth the glory of God. Faith is always at peace, undisturbed no matter what happens. The waves may be terrible, the wind blowing hard, as when Jesus and His disciples were on the boat in the storm. (See Mark 4:36–41.) Jesus was asleep during the storm, and the disciples cried out to him, *"Teacher, do You not care that we are perishing?"* (v. 38). He spoke, and there was a great calm! Then He said to His disciples, *"Why are you so fearful? How is it that you have no faith?"* (v. 40). Jesus Christ is *"the author and finisher of our faith"* (Heb. 12:2), the divine authority with inspiration. We preach this word of faith to bring forth to the world the touch of heaven.

The Lord is in this place. He is here to revive, to fill, to change, to express, to give power *"over all the power of the enemy"* (Luke 10:19).

There is therefore now no condemnation to those who are in Christ Jesus, who do not walk according to the flesh, but according to the Spirit. For the law of the Spirit of life in Christ Jesus has made me free from the law of sin and death. (Rom. 8:1–2)

A New Epoch—A Divine Vocation

Life came out of death because of the Cross, and then came resurrection, a manifestation of the operation of God. I was dead in trespasses and sins, and now I am alive unto God (Eph. 2:1). I have eternal life.

He opens the prison doors to all who believe, and by faith we enter in. He *"became for us... righteousness"* (1 Cor. 1:30), and we are one with Him forever. Heirship and joint heirship have been made possible for us by His death, resurrection, and ascension (Rom. 8:17).

"There is therefore now no condemnation to those who are in Christ Jesus" (v. 1). There is no cloud, nothing between us and God. Oh, the thrill of it! We are *"hidden with Christ in God"* (Col. 3:3)—immersed, covered—and nothing can break through. It is by the grace of God that we are here, and as sure as we are here, we will be there, *"receiving a kingdom which cannot be shaken"* (Heb. 12:28), *"for our God is a consuming fire"* (v. 29). There is something very beautiful about being in Christ in God, ready for everything— ready!

God *"has begotten us again to a living hope"* (1 Pet. 1:3) in order to make us like Himself. The radiance of the divine makes a new creation. *"The law of the Spirit of life in Christ Jesus* [makes us] *free from the law of sin and death"* (Rom. 8:2). The quickening Spirit, fellow-heirs, a divine flow—white heat, full, holy, inflammable, causing others to catch fire— quickening, no condemnation. Do you know these things? Glory! This is a magnificent conception of our eternal relationship: catching the rays of divine glory, a changing all the time. We are ready because of the intensity of the fire within! Jesus is manifested in our flesh (2 Cor. 4:11), ruling and reigning until the rivers flow and the floodtide is here, bringing life, life to all.

Filled with the Holy Spirit,
Has He come?
Does He abide?

I know the Lord's laid His hand on me,
I know the Lord's laid His hand on me.
He fills me with the Holy Spirit,
I know the Lord's laid His hand on me.

Filled! A flowing, quickening, moving flame of God.

We are *"not drunk with wine,...but...filled with the Spirit"* (Eph. 5:18 KJV), more and more filled with this life, this great expansiveness of God's gifts, graces, and beatitudes, which is changing us all the time, moving us on to greater enlargement in the Spirit.

God is with you. The Spirit of the Lord is upon you. Count on Him. Be a chosen vessel in fellowship with God for this day. If you in any way fail to be filled, some need will be unmet. God makes the opportunity for the person who is ready. The Bible is our all. There God reveals His plan and feeds us. Those who trust in Him will never be put to shame (Ps. 22:5; 1 Pet. 2:6).

We cannot be ordinary people; God must be glorified in us. Some say, "If I could only feel the power!" Do not pay any attention to what you feel if you are moved to act in a situation of need. Act in the authority of the power. God makes the opportunity when we are in the place of being hidden in God, of being *"hidden with Christ in God"* (Col. 3:3). *"The law of the Spirit of life"* (Rom. 8:2) is opposed to death and disease; it is the opposite of what is earthly, for within us is a heavenly production. Fresh desire for God's glory makes us ready for the place of opportunity. *"Our God is a consuming fire"* (Heb. 12:29). The cross is empty and Jesus is glorified through us. He is risen, and rivers of white heat are flowing.

"Multitudes, multitudes in the valley of decision! For the day of the LORD is near in the valley of decision" (Joel 3:14). Decide, and the floods will appear. Faith is the victory, for faith is substance and evidence (Heb. 11:1).

The Hearing of Faith

Praise the Lord; praise the Lord. *"Only believe"* (Mark 5:36). All things are possible, only believe (Mark 9:23). We are to be absolutely dependent on God alone, on His grand will. *"Only believe."*

"What then shall we say that Abraham our father has found according to the flesh?" (Rom. 4:1). He found something wonderful through God the Holy Spirit. Also, considering the fact that all flesh is like grass (Isa. 40:6), and that *"in me (that is, in my flesh) nothing good dwells"* (Rom. 7:18), what has Abraham, our father, found? Only this: that, for the believer, God has One who can live in the flesh, who can hold the flesh, by the power of God, above sin and judgment.

Jesus Christ is the center of the life where the body, the flesh, has come to the place of being inhabited by God, where God, dwelling in these earthly temples, can live and reign supreme. He has made alive what was dead, bringing *"life and immortality to light through the gospel"* (2 Tim. 1:10), and the Son of God is manifested there.

God has wonderful things for us. Many days in the past have been wonderful, but no day is like the present—the Holy Spirit lifting us into His presence, the power flowing, our whole being flaming with the glory of God. This is God's divine plan for humanity when the Holy Spirit has come. Today, we are nearer to the goal; the vision is clearer, the Holy Spirit bringing us into the treasure of the Most High. What did our father Abraham have? I depend upon the Holy Spirit to bring us into revelation concerning this. There is no room for weakness if we see this mighty incoming life through the Spirit.

OBEYING GOD

"What then shall we say that Abraham our father has found according to the flesh?" (Rom. 4:1). He found that, as he heard the voice of God and obeyed it, it did not only judge him, but wonderful things were also manifested. One day, long ago, God said to Abraham, "Come out." (See Genesis 12:1–4.) God has wonderful things to say to you if you come to the hearing of faith, not to the hearing of the natural order, taste, desire, or affection. Oh yes, if God gets your ear, you will come out.

One day, God said to me, also, "Come out." I was in the Wesleyan Church; I had not been in it for long. Was there anything wrong with the Wesleyan Church? No. Only, God said, "Come out." He had something further for me. The Salvation Army was in full swing at that time. I was very anxious to get the best. Revival was in full swing there, but then the Salvation Army turned to other things. So God again said to me, "Come out." We need to have the hearing of faith, always soaring higher, understanding the leading of the Spirit. Oh, the Breath of God! Then I went to the Brethren. They had the Word, but they had so much of the letter of the law with it (see Romans 7:6; 2 Corinthians 3:6); they split hairs over too many things. And God again said to me, "Come out." "Oh," people said, "he has gone again; there is no satisfying him." Then came the baptism of the Holy Spirit, *"with signs following"* (Mark 16:20 KJV), according to Acts 2—God alone speaking, faith bringing us to a place of revelation to cover us, God coming in and manifesting His power.

BELIEVING AND ACTING ON THE WORD

"What then shall we say that Abraham our father has found according to the flesh?" (Rom. 4:1). He found two things: first, a righteousness by law; and second, a righteousness by faith. That is, believing what God says, and daring to act on the authority of God's Word. God will meet us there, within that blessed place, making opportunities of blessing for us—love, truth, revelation, manifestation—God and us in activity, bringing divine ability and activity into action.

> Oh, it's all right now,
> It's all right now,
> For Jesus is my Savior,
> So it's all right now.

The way into the treasure-house of the Most High is the authority of the living Word. The kingdom of heaven is open to all believers. God has called us, bringing us into divine association with heaven, if we will dare to believe, for *"all things are possible to him who believes"* (Mark 9:23).

When we believe, we will find, like Abraham who believed God, tremendous ability—weakness changed into strength, character, power, association within; *all things* [made] *new"* (Rev. 21:5). We will find a life yielded, absorbed by divine authority, standing on the principles of God.

In Wellington, New Zealand, a crowd of needy people had come for help at one of my meetings, and among them was a heavyset woman. God revealed to me the presence of the Enemy within her body. She cried out, "You are killing me," and fell down in the aisle. I said, "Lift her up. God has not finished yet." The onlookers who were judging us over this case didn't know, but just three yards from them, she was loosed from a cancer.

It is wise to believe God. God has a place for the man or woman who dares to believe. The one whom God has His hand on is not subject to the opinions of others. Our father Abraham discovered this. May God increase the number who dare to believe under all circumstances, who dare to believe God on the authority of the Word.

I once came across a peculiar case. A man was bent double; he was in agony, having cancer of the bladder, and he cried and cried. I said, "Do you believe God?" He said, "No, I have nothing in common with God." I tried to bring him to the place of believing, but his mental capacity was affected. I said, "I see that you don't understand; it may be that God wants me to help you." I said, "What is the name of Jesus? It is the name of the One who met us at Calvary, who has come with new life divine."

Believe all the message; God intends us to be an extraordinary people with this wonderful life of faith in the body. Abraham found, when he believed

God, that by faith he was bound to almighty power, equipped for service.

Laying my hands on the sick man in the name of Jesus, I didn't have to say, "Are you whole?" He knew he was whole. He couldn't tell what he had received. This man had been interested in yachts; he was a member of a yacht club. His friends went as usual to see him and began talking about yachts. He said, "Yachts! Yachts! Talk to me about Jesus!"

Oh, yes, there is something in the name of Jesus. Our father Abraham found it. The Word of God is the link, the key, the personality of divine equipping. There is something mighty in believing God. Have you found it? Have you found a faith that believes God, that apprehends what God has said? What did God say? God said that because Abraham believed Him, He would cover him with His righteousness, holiness, integrity of faith. (See Genesis 15:6.) God loves to see His children when they believe Him. He covers them. It is a lovely covering, the covering of the Almighty. Blessed is the man to whom God imputes righteousness (Rom. 4:6). Is it to be so in your life?

God has a perfect work for us, a hearing of faith. When we have the hearing of faith, we are within the sound of His voice, and when we hear Him speak, we find that our own speech betrays us. With this hearing of faith, we are epistles of the divine character (see 2 Corinthians 3:2–3), having His life, passion, and compassion. Beloved, there must be this divine fellowship between us and God.

The people asked Jesus, *"What shall we do, that we may work the works of God?"* (John 6:28). Jesus answered, *"This is the work of God, that you believe in Him whom He sent"* (v. 29).

CHRIST DWELLING WITHIN BY FAITH

This is what our father Abraham found: he became a written epistle, *"known and read by all men"* (2 Cor. 3:2). Paul was delighted with being an epistle of Christ; he followed this divine fire with all *"those who are of the faith of Abraham"* (Rom. 4:16). When we read what Paul wrote in Ephesians and Colossians, we see what he, with Abraham, had received: *"Christ in you, the hope of glory"* (Col. 1:27). Everything we need is embedded within us; we are *"filled with all the fullness of God"* (Eph. 3:19).

The baptism in the Holy Spirit crowns Jesus King in His royal palace within us. When the King is crowned, what tremendous things we find pertaining to our flesh: perpetual divine motion, the power of God sweeping through the regions of weakness. What have we received pertaining to our flesh? New life flowing through it. All the Word of God is *"Yes, and...Amen"* (2 Cor. 1:20) to faith. We receive mighty, divine actions in the human frame, which are so full of divine operation that we see God working. I see such possibilities for young men and women who come into line with God; nothing can interfere with the progress of God, the Author of Life (see Hebrews 5:9) and the Finisher of Faith (Heb. 12:2). Never be afraid of your voice when the Spirit is upon you, nor of how you live your life when you are operating in the ministry of freedom.

"No one can say that Jesus is Lord except by the Holy Spirit" (1 Cor. 12:3). In the truth of this verse, I see the dew of the Spirit (see Psalm 133:3), the order of blessing, the ability to crown Jesus King, being set apart for God.

Then there is the sealing of the Spirit (2 Cor. 1:22; Eph. 1:13), the great adjusting, giving us knowledge in the revelation of Jesus as King over all; all our affections, desires, and wishes are His.

We receive His compassion, His meekness, His dynamic, the power to move the Devil away. We live in a big plan, a force of unity, a divine capacity, making things move.

A man and his wife came to me troubled about things that were taking place in the meetings they were holding. I said, "You two can be so perfectly joined in unity that you can take the victory in every meeting. Not a thing can stand against you; you can have a perfect fellowship in Christ, which the Devil is not able to break. *'If two of you agree on earth concerning anything that they ask, it will be done for them by My Father in heaven'* (Matt. 18:19). Dare, on the authority of God's Word, to bind every evil spirit in the meeting."

We have a faith manifested in our human bodies, a *"circumcision of Christ"* (Col. 2:11; see also Romans 2:29; Philippians 3:3) for our home life, financial difficulties, and the like. We are *"more than conquerors"* (Rom. 8:37) in this operation of faith.

> *It is of faith that it might be according to grace, so that the promise might be sure to all the seed, not only to those who are of the law, but also to those who are of the faith of Abraham, who is the father of us all.* (Rom. 4:16)

Nothing is as large, inhabited by this operation of faith, that is brought to us through Calvary. I feel mighty revival coming; my whole being moves toward it. I dare to believe in simplicity of faith.

Once, in Norway, the halls were packed, and people thronged the streets wanting to hear God's

Word. We want the same thing to happen in London. God has given us a divine plan to operate with Him. The deluge can come—a Pentecostal outpouring for the glory of God.

There is now a way into the kingdom of heaven by faith. God is not holding back; we only have to believe in order to see the mighty power of God fall, and I am here to awaken you to this.

THE TESTING OF OUR FAITH

Abraham was tested. Yet God is greater than our testing, and He opens a door of deliverance. Faith! God never changes. What had Abraham received? Testing. But he was called, chosen, and faithful. He was faithful to God in the trial. For twenty-five years, Abraham waited for the promise of a son to be fulfilled. He believed *"contrary to hope"* (Rom. 4:18), *"giving glory to God"* (v. 20). Not one thing will fail if you dare to believe. All fullness in manifestation will arise through faith; all needs of the body will be met in a moment on the word of faith. Give God the glory. Stuttering, tuberculosis, neurasthenia, need of salvation—all needs will be met if we dare to believe. We are in the place of receiving all that our father Abraham received. Let us put in our claim, letting the deluge come, which God wants to send.

WHAT GOD HAS PROMISED, HE IS ABLE TO PERFORM

Let us be *"strengthened in faith, giving glory to God, and being fully convinced that what He* [has] *promised He* [is] *also able to perform"* (Rom. 4:20–21).

Then God will be glorified in us and we in Him (2 Thess. 1:12), because we will have found, as Abraham did, the hearing of faith, the righteousness that is ours through faith. Amen.

Faith: The Substance

L et us read from Hebrews 11. This chapter contains one of the greatest subjects there is from Genesis to Revelation. It is impossible to bring to you anything greater than the nature of God. We have now entered into not the covenant but the very nature of God, the divine nature, through faith. God has all thoughts and all knowledge, and we may have glimpses of His divine life. The Word of God is life. Jesus, the Word, became flesh (John 1:14); He came in the flesh for the very purpose of moving people. Yes, beloved, the Creator was in the midst of creation. He opened blind eyes, unstopped deaf ears, and made the lame walk; but He had all knowledge.

We experience the new birth as much as we allow natural things to cease; then He comes in, in all His fullness. If He comes in, the *"old man"* (Rom. 6:6) goes out. Now, I believe this morning's plan is for us all, but we must get into the real spirit of it. Beloved, do not stumble if you cannot move mountains; oh, no, there may be some molehills that need moving first. *"He who is in you is greater than he who is in the world"* (1 John 4:4). God has no need of a person who is hot today and cold tomorrow; He needs people who are hot today and hotter tomorrow and still hotter the next day, for they are the ones who are going to touch the glory. The Lord never changes; He is always the same (Heb. 13:8). If you change, it does not mean that God has changed. I am amazed all the time at what God is doing—it is *"from glory to glory"* (2 Cor. 3:18).

THE FOUNDATION OF THE WORD OF GOD

Now, it is no good unless we have a foundation, but, glory to God, our foundation is the most powerful and unmovable foundation; it is the very Word of God. When we are born again, we are born of a *"substance"* (Heb. 11:1), the Word of God; there is no corruption in it. It is the incorruptible Word of God (1 Pet. 1:23). I believe that when a person is born again, he receives knowledge with respect to how to sow the Word of God so that it will bring another into the same knowledge. Everyone who is born again can sow.

When Jesus said, *"God so loved the world that He gave His only begotten Son, that whoever believes in Him should not perish but have everlasting life"* (John 3:16), it was an immeasurable sowing. It's a fact that is worked within us and has to come out; but it is the plan of God, and you are all in it. I believe that there can be an enlargement in us such as will swallow us up, and if you are not in that place, then you must take a back seat. But remember this, we all have more than we are using.

We must build ourselves up in our *"most holy faith"* (Jude 20). Do not stop running in the race of faith; it is an awful thing for a person to run and then stop, and for someone else to get the prize. Paul spoke

40

about this in 1 Corinthians 9:24: *"Do you not know that those who run in a race all run, but one receives the prize? Run in such a way that you may obtain it."* He also said, in Philippians 3:12, *"Not that I have already attained, or am already perfected; but I press on, that I may lay hold of that for which Christ Jesus has also laid hold of me."* Therefore, Paul cried out, *"I **press** toward the goal"* (v. 14, emphasis added). It is a disgrace to God for a person just to keep pace. We must press on. If you are making no headway, you must be a backslider, because you have had such opportunities.

"THE EVIDENCE OF THINGS NOT SEEN"

Now I want to dwell a little on the word *"substance."* *"Substance"* is *"the evidence of things not seen"* (Heb. 11:1). In every born-again person, there is a power that is greater than the natural force. God says twice in one chapter, *"Lay hold on eternal life"* (1 Tim. 6:12, 19). Eternal life is something we cannot see, and yet we have to lay hold of it.

Now, beloved, we must proceed farther than we ever have before. I really mean all I say. I am not speaking from the abundance of my mind, but of my heart. The abundance of the mind makes for swelled heads, but we want swelled hearts. I want to make you all drunk with *"new wine"* (Matt. 9:17). We can *"have this treasure in earthen vessels"* (2 Cor. 4:7). God does not want you to be natural people. He wants you to be people who will cut through anything. He wants you to be born into His life. The new birth is life, the life of God. *"Christ in you, the hope of glory"* (Col. 1:27). No person can go on in this way and stand still. Love the Word of God. *"In the beginning was the*

Word, and the Word was with God, and the Word was God" (John 1:1). Jesus was *"the only begotten of the Father, full of grace and truth"* (v. 14).

Perhaps you have never before known what God wants you to possess. Now take these words: *"By faith we understand that the worlds were framed by the word of God, so that the things which are seen were not made of things which are visible"* (Heb. 11:3). My word, if you do not all become "big" today—I do not mean in your own estimation!

Now, when you first came into the world, you were made, but when you were born again, you were *"begotten"* (1 Pet. 1:3). Read John 1:1–3:

> *In the beginning was the Word, and the Word was with God, and the Word was God. He was in the beginning with God. All things were made through Him, and without Him nothing was made that was made.*

So you see, all things were made by Him. Oh, beloved, He will act if you will let Him have a chance. What do I mean? Well, listen! A man came to me and said, "Can you help me? I cannot sleep, and my nerves are in terrible shape."

Now, Jesus put a principle in the Word of God. He said, "Ask anything in My name, and I will do it." (See John 14:13–14.) So I prayed for the man, and said, "Now go home and sleep in the name of Jesus." He protested, "But I can't sleep," and I said, "Go home and sleep," and I gave him a push. So he left, and according to the Word of God, he went home and slept. He slept for so long that his wife went to wake him up, but, thinking he was tired, let him sleep on. But he slept all of Saturday, and his poor wife did not know what to do. However, the man awoke, and he was so changed that he got up and went about shouting, "I am a new man; praise the Lord!"

What had done it? Why, it was the Word of God, and we have the Word in us, *the faith of the Son of God*" (Gal. 2:20 KJV). Now, we can all have from God what we believe for. If you want anything, put your hand up. If you are in earnest, walk down to the front. And if you are really desperate, run down. Amen.

6

Ambition Realized— Desire Fulfilled

L ike precious faith" (2 Pet. 1:1). What would happen to us and to the needs of the world if we would get to the place where we could believe God? May God give us the desire. Faith is a tremendous power, an inward mover. We have not yet seen all that God has for us.

When I was a little boy, I remember at times asking my father for a penny's worth of something. He would not give it to me at first. So I would sit down by his side, and every now and then I would touch him ever so gently, saying, "Father, Father." My mother would say to my father, "Why don't you answer the child?" My father would reply, "I have done so." But still I would remain seated next to him, saying, "Father, Father, Father," ever so quietly. Then, if he went into the garden, I would follow him. I would just touch his sleeve and say, "Father, Father!" Did I ever go away without the accomplishment of my desire? No, not once. In a similar way, let God have His way with us. Let God fulfill His great desire for purity of heart within us, so *"that Christ may dwell in* [our] *hearts through faith"* (Eph. 3:17), and so that the might of God's Spirit may accompany our ministry. Let us be filled with divine enthusiasm, with rivers flowing.

PRECIOUS FAITH

"To those who have obtained like precious faith" (2 Pet. 1:1)—a faith of divine origin, springing up in our hearts. Our foundation is tested in a time of strain, for the outside must be as the inside. It is good to have the Holy Spirit, but the sun inside must give a brilliancy outside. Faith! *"Like precious faith"* is greater than the mind or body or any activity. Faith is a living power revealed in you. The moment you believe, you have that for which you are believing. For faith is *"substance"* and *"evidence"* (Heb. 11:1).

You were not saved by feelings or experiences. You were saved by the power of God the moment you believed the Word of God. God came in by His Word and laid the foundation. Faith shattered the old life-nature by the power of God; it shattered the old life by the Word of God.

We must come to God's Book. His Word is our foundation. When we speak of the Word, we speak of almighty power, a substance of rich dynamite diffusing through the human, displaying its might, and bringing everything else into insignificance. The Word of God is formed within our bodies—*"the temple of the Holy Spirit"* (1 Cor. 6:19)—a living principle laid down of rock. The Word of the living God is formed in us—mighty in thought, language, activity, movement, and anointing, a fire mightier than dynamite and able to resist the mightiest pressure the Devil can bring against it.

In these eventful days, we must have nothing that is ordinary. We must have what is extraordinary, allowing God, by His wonderful revelations, to display His gifts and graces in our hearts for the deliverance of others. Peter said, *"To those who have obtained like precious faith"* (2 Pet. 1:1); it was the same kind of faith that Abraham had. Have the faith of God. Because we are born again, a supernatural power works within us. We have the unique peace of God, and are working with a changed vision; we are more wonderful than we know.

Peter said to the lame man, *"Silver and gold I do not have, but what I do have I give you: in the name of Jesus Christ of Nazareth, rise up and walk"* (Acts 3:6). There was operation and manifestation, and the man was healed. Faith! *"Like precious faith."* It is all of the same material: belief in God's Word. Noah had faith that was tested. Abraham had faith, and all the prophets had one fact working: faith!

GOD HAS NO LIMITATION

The patriarchs and prophets had limitations, but God has come to us with no limitation, *"exceedingly abundantly above all that we ask or think"* (Eph. 3:20). There have been memorable days when the Holy Spirit has come. When I was twenty-one years old, God flooded my life with His power, and there has not been a day since without wonderful things happening.

God, by His divine power, is flooding human vessels. God is being made manifest in the flesh, in our flesh. Christ is being made manifest by the power of God. God has chosen a new way for us. He Himself has made us *"kings and priests"* (Rev. 1:6; 5:10), and the day is not far distant when we will be with Him forever.

The Holy Spirit could not have come unless Jesus came first. The Holy Spirit crowns Him King, and all of His power is to be manifested through us. How?

Interpretation of Tongues

Rivers of living water. The man divinely operated, discerning the mind of Christ without measure. To live, to drink, to sup, to walk, to talk with Him.

> Oh, 'tis all right now,
> Oh, 'tis all right now,
> For Jesus is a friend of mine
> And 'tis all right now.

FAITH AND THE WORD

But Jesus must come in first; all God's fullness is in Him (Col. 2:9). All God's revelation is in Him. The life of God comes into us by faith. *"Precious faith"* is an eternal process of working; it has no end, but it has a beginning: *"faith comes by hearing, and hearing by the word of God"* (Rom. 10:17). Faith forms things of eternal forces in our human nature. Faith, God's embrace, is the grip of almightiness. What is faith? It is the eternal nature of God; it can never decay or fade away; it is with you all the way of your spiritual journey, and will end in eternal day.

Faith is the Word (Rom. 10:8). *"There are three that bear witness in heaven: the Father, the Word, and the Holy Spirit; and these three are one"* (1 John 5:7). Faith has so many springs. *"Forever, O LORD, Your word is settled in heaven"* (Ps. 119:89). We have only *"a shadow of things to come"* (Col. 2:17).

Be a person of desire, hungry and thirsty. Don't be satisfied. I cannot move on faith unless it is better than my mind, greater than I am. No one is made on "trailing clouds of glory"; we are made in hard places, at Wits' End Corner, with no way out. A man is made in adversity. David said, "In my distress, God brought me to an enlarged place; I was set free, and He helped me." (See Psalm 4:1; 18:36 KJV.)

Eight years ago, after a distressing voyage, I went straight from the ship to a meeting. As I entered the building, a man fell down across the doorway in a fit. The Spirit of the Lord was upon me, and I commanded the evil spirit to leave. In my visit this year, I ventured to ask, "Does anyone remember that incident?" I spoke in English. The man did not know a word of English; however, he stood up. I told him to come to the platform. He said he knew the binding power of the name of Jesus, and that he had not had a fit since the "stranger" had come. That healing occurred because I knew Acts 1:1: *"Jesus began both to do and teach."* I began to do, the man was healed, and then I could teach the people. Oh, my God, keep me there!

In Palestine, at the Damascus Gate, and on the Mount of Olives, I saw men baptized with the Holy Spirit as in Acts 2. Begin to do, and then to preach. God is always waiting to manifest His divine power. God intends us to begin.

BE A COMMUNICATOR OF DIVINE LIFE

Be a communicator of divine life for others. His divine power has called us to glory and virtue. (See 2

Peter 1:3 KJV.) My wife used to say, "He giveth grace and glory, too." Oh, beloved, receive power! Believe for the power of the Lord to be so manifested through your body that, as people touch you, they are healed. Then there will be the illumination of the power of the Life! Believe for the current to go through you to others. It is amazing what can happen when there is an urgent need; and God can arrange for an urgent need, where there is no time to pray, only to act. The person who is filled with the Holy Spirit lives in an act. I come with the life of the risen Christ, my mouth under the anointing of the Holy Spirit, my mind operative to live and act in the power of the Spirit. We must so live in God that we claim an enlarging in the wisdom of God.

At one place where I ministered, there were six thousand people outside the building, poor things in wheelchairs, and as I went laying my hands on them, they were healed; as they were touched, they were made whole. This faith means an increase in the knowledge of God and the righteousness of Christ, a life filled with God, His mantle upon you with grace multiplied. God did this for Abraham, and added blessing onto blessing. *"Blessed are those who hear the word of God and keep it!"* (Luke 11:28).

The people asked Jesus, *"What shall we do, that we may work the works of God?"* (John 6:28). Jesus answered, *"Believe in Him whom He sent"* (v. 29). Jesus also said, *"He who believes in Me, the works that I do he will do also; and greater works than these he will do, because I go to My Father"* (John 14:12). Faith sees the glory of Another, and it is revealed *"from faith to faith"* (Rom. 1:17). You may increase wonderfully before I see you again.

When I was in Örebro, Sweden, eight years ago, I ministered to a twelve-year-old blind girl; when I visited this time, they told me she has had perfect sight from that day. I never knew it; it is after I leave that testimonies come.

> *Whoever says to this mountain, "Be removed and be cast into the sea," and does not doubt in his heart, but believes that those things he says will be done, he will have whatever he says. Therefore I say to you, whatever things you ask when you pray, believe that you receive them, and you will have them.* (Mark 11:23–24)

Have faith in God! If I believe, then what? I receive what I wish, as I begin to speak. God brings it to pass—not just with a fig tree, but even with a mountain (see Matthew 21:19–22)—whatever you say.

Let me repeat a testimony to illustrate a point. In one place where I was ministering, a man said, "You have helped everyone but me." I said, "What is the trouble?" He answered, "I cannot sleep; I am losing my reason!" He had not slept much for three years, until he got in such a state that when he was shaving, an evil spirit would say, "Life is not worth living," and at times the man had almost killed himself. Whenever he was near the water, the evil spirit would say, "Jump in; jump in, and end it; it is not worth it." Then he came to one of my meetings and heard that he could be delivered. He came up to me and said, "I cannot sleep." So I said, "There is no need to go anywhere else for help; believe! According to the Word of God, go home and sleep in the name of Jesus." He returned and testified, "I can sleep anywhere. I sleep, sleep, sleep, and God has saved me."

There are nine fruits of the Spirit (Gal. 5:22–23) and nine gifts of the Spirit (1 Cor. 12:7–10). Wisdom is coupled with love, knowledge with joy, and faith with peace. Examine yourselves—are you in peace? God is delighted when we are in peace, so I said to the brother, "Go home and sleep, and I will believe God." This man went home, and his wife said, "Well, did you see him?" He said, "He helped everyone but me." However, he fell asleep. Later, his wife said, "I wonder if he is all right," for morning, noon, and night, he was still asleep. Then he awoke bright and happy, rested and restored.

What did it? Belief in God—then speaking. *"He will have whatever he says"* (Mark 11:23). Do you have this *"like precious faith"* (2 Pet. 1:1)? Deal bountifully with the oppressed. *"Everyone who asks receives"* (Matt. 7:8). Ask, and it is done. Live for God. Keep clean and holy. Live in God's anointing, in God's desires and plans. Glorify Him in the establishment of blessing for the people—seeing God's glory manifested in the midst. Amen.

Be Wide Awake

*Now it came to pass, when Jesus finished
commanding His twelve disciples, that He departed
from there to teach and to preach in their cities. And
when John had heard in prison about the works of
Christ, he sent two of his disciples and said to Him,
"Are You the Coming One, or do we look for another?"
Jesus answered and said to them, "Go and tell John
the things which you hear and see: the blind see
and the lame walk; the lepers are cleansed and the
deaf hear; the dead are raised up and the poor have
the gospel preached to them. And blessed is he who
is not offended because of Me." As they departed,
Jesus began to say to the multitudes concerning John:
"What did you go out into the wilderness to see? A
reed shaken by the wind? But what did you go out to
see? A man clothed in soft garments? Indeed, those
who wear soft clothing are in kings' houses. But what
did you go out to see? A prophet? Yes, I say to you,
and more than a prophet. For this is he of whom
it is written: 'Behold, I send My messenger before
Your face, who will prepare Your way before You.'*

Assuredly, I say to you, among those born of women there has not risen one greater than John the Baptist; but he who is least in the kingdom of heaven is greater than he. And from the days of John the Baptist until now the kingdom of heaven suffers violence, and the violent take it by force."
—Matthew 11:1–12

Faith brings into action a principle within our hearts, so that Christ can dethrone every power of Satan. God's accomplishment for us can be proved in our experience. We are not in a dormant position, but we have a power, a revelation, a life. Oh, the greatness of it! How great are the possibilities of man in the hand of God, brought out in revelation and force!

John the Baptist had a wonderful revelation, a mighty anointing. How the power of God rested upon him! All Israel was moved. Jesus said, *"There has not risen one greater than John the Baptist; but he who is least in the kingdom of heaven is greater than he."*

In this passage, we see how satanic power can blind our minds unless we are filled or insulated by the power of God. Satan suggests to John, "Don't you think you have made a mistake? Is Jesus really the Messiah?" I find that men who might be used by God to subdue kingdoms are defeated by allowing the suggestions of Satan to dethrone their better knowledge of the power of God. So John sent two of his disciples to Jesus, asking, *"Are You the Coming One, or do we look for another?"* Jesus said, *"Go and tell John the things which you hear and see."* And when they saw the miracles and wonders, they were ready.

Jesus asked the multitudes who were with Him, *"What did you go out into the wilderness to see? A reed shaken by the wind?"* No; God wants men to be flames of fire (Ps. 104:4), *"strong in the Lord and in the power of His might"* (Eph. 6:10). Let us live as those who have seen the King, having a resurrection touch. We know we are sons of God as we believe His Word and stand in the truth of it. (See John 1:12; Philippians 2:15–16.)

Interpretation of Tongues
The Spirit of the Lord breathes upon the bones and upon the "things that are not," and changes them in a moment, making the weak strong, quickening what is dead into life.

THE KINGDOM OF HEAVEN

The kingdom of heaven is within us; it is the Christ, the Word of God. *"The kingdom of heaven suffers violence."* How does the kingdom suffer violence? Whenever anyone is suffering, whenever someone has paralysis, if you feel distress in any way, it means that the kingdom is suffering violence at the hands of the Adversary. Could the kingdom of heaven bring weakness, disease, tuberculosis, cancers, tumors? The kingdom of God is within you; it is the life of Jesus, the power of the Highest. It is pure, holy; it has no disease or imperfection. But Satan comes *"to steal, and to kill, and to destroy"* (John 10:10).

I know of a beautiful nine-year-old girl who was possessed by an evil spirit; she screamed and moaned for years. The neighbors complained, but the father said, "These hands will work, but my child will never go to an asylum."

One day, I went to this home, and the Spirit of the Lord came upon me. I took hold of the child, looked right into her eyes, and said, "You evil spirit, come out, in the name of Jesus." She went to a couch and fell asleep, and from that day, she was perfect. I know deliverance came, but I want you to see the wiles of Satan and the reality of dethroning evil powers in the name of Jesus—the almightiness of God against the might of Satan.

DO NOT BE ASLEEP!

Oh, do not be asleep concerning the deep things of God! Have a flaming indignation against the power of Satan. Lot had a righteous indignation, but too late (see 2 Peter 2:7–8); he should have had it when he went into Sodom in the first place. Be thankful that you are alive to hear, and that God can change situations. We all have a greater audacity of faith and fact to reach.

Fools, because of their iniquity, are afflicted; they draw near to death, and then they cry to the Lord in their trouble, and He heals them and delivers them out of their distresses. (See Psalm 107:17–20.) Catch faith by the grace of God, and be delivered. Anything that takes me from an attitude of worship, peace, and joy, of consciousness of God's presence, has a satanic source. *"He who is in you is greater than he who is in the world"* (1 John 4:4).

Is there anyone here suffering? (A young man steps out into the aisle.) Are you saved? "I am." Do you believe that the kingdom of God is within you? "I do." Now, young man, say, "In Jesus' name, come out of my leg, you evil power!" Are you free? "Yes."

Oh, people, put the Bible into practice and claim your blood-bought rights! Every step of my way since I received the baptism of the Holy Spirit, I have paid the price for others, letting God take me through, so that I might show people how to become free. Some say, "I am seeking the baptism, and I am having such a struggle; is it not strange?" No; God is preparing you to help somebody else.

The reason I am so rigid on the necessity of receiving the baptism of the Spirit is that I fought it out myself. I could have asked anybody, but God was preparing me to help others. The power of God fell on me. I could not satisfy or express the joy within as the Spirit spoke through me in tongues. I had had anointings before, but when the fullness came with a high tide, I knew it was the baptism; but God had to show me.

There is a difference between having the gift of tongues (see 1 Corinthians 12:7–11) and speaking as the Spirit gives utterance (Acts 2:4); the Holy Spirit uses the gift. If I could make every person who has a bad leg so annoyed with the Devil that he would kick the other leg, we could accomplish something. When I say this, I am only exaggerating to wake you up.

Many times I have been shut in with insane people, praying for their deliverance. The demon power would come and bite, but I never gave in. It would dethrone a higher principle if I gave in. It is the inward presence of God that suffers violence at the hands of Satan, *"and the violent take it by force."* By the grace of God, we are to understand that we are to keep authority over our bodies, making them subject to the higher power—to God's mighty provision for sinful humanity.

> Jesus paid it all,
> All to Him I owe;
> Sin had left a crimson stain,
> He washed it white as snow.

Faith: A Living Power

But without faith it is impossible to please Him,
for he who comes to God must believe that He is,
and that He is a rewarder of those
who diligently seek Him.
—Hebrews 11:6

The substance of all things is in this verse, I think—no, I am sure, because a preacher should preach only what he is sure of. Anybody can think, but a preacher should say what he knows, and I am going to preach what I know. That is a wonderful position to be in, so we have a great subject this morning. We must understand nothing less than this: we have to be the *"epistle of Christ"* (2 Cor. 3:3), a living word, a living faith, equipped with the revelation of the plan of the future. *"In Him all things consist"* (Col. 1:17).

Faith is a reality. It is not something that you can handle, but something that handles you to handle others. I am living in the inheritance of it because of the faith of God. It is a gift of God (Eph. 2:8).

Through faith, the eternal Word brings forth life in our hearts by the operation of His Spirit, and we realize we are living in a divine order, where God is manifesting His power and living with us. This is the plan of God for us, our inheritance, that the world should receive a blessing through us.

God has come within us, living in us with a divine life. Everyone, without exception, will go away from here with a new vision, a new Book, so that we may go forth because of the Word.

The Lord has one great plan, and that is to reveal to us that we are so much greater than we know; you are a thousand times greater than you have any idea of. The Word of the Lord will reveal that all things are possible if you will dare to believe (Mark 9:23), and that signs and wonders are within reach of all of us. The Lord wishes me to make it known that you do not have to go up or down to find Him. He, the Word of Life, is in your hearts. (See Romans 10:6–10.) I perceive that the Lord has this treasure within us so *"that the excellence of the power"* will bring glory to God (2 Cor. 4:7).

We have become *"partakers of the divine nature"* (2 Pet. 1:4). The moment you believe, you are *"begotten...* [with] *a living hope"* (1 Pet. 1:3), a new power, the power to lay hold of impossibilities and to make them possible. Do you want this? The people said to Jesus, *"Give us this bread always"* (John 6:34). They were enamored with Him. Life forever, real life, eternal life—for the person who comes into this association with the Lord, this is beyond all his earthly measurement. You will need a heavenly measure to measure this.

I am very hungry for your sake today. I have seen the possibilities of every person in Christ. I must show you that, by the grace of God, it is impossible to fail, no matter what the circumstances. This knowledge of the truth that you have within you is so remarkable that it will put you in a place where failure cannot exist. You will see the power of God manifest in your midst. If I were to speak with any less truth than this, it would be of no value, for this is the greatest truth of all: I am saved by a new life, by the Word of the Lord, by the living Christ. I become associated with *"a new creation"* (2 Cor. 5:17), and He continually takes me into new revelations.

FAITH AND THE WORD OF GOD

Let us compare two passages of Scripture:

By faith we understand that the worlds were framed by the word of God, so that the things which are seen were not made of things which are visible. (Heb. 11:3)

In the beginning was the Word, and the Word was with God, and the Word was God. He was in the beginning with God. All things were made through Him, and without Him nothing was made that was made. (John 1:1–3)

Nothing is made without the Word of God. Peter said, "I am begotten with this Word." (See 1 Peter 1:3.) There is something within me that has almighty power within it, if I dare to believe it. It is heavenly treasure (Matt. 13:44), and it is called the substance of faith. (See Hebrews 11:1.)

Praise the Lord, you must realize that God is within you as a mighty power, enabling you to act so that signs and wonders may be made manifest; this is the great purpose. Have we believed just in order to get to heaven? No, we must also be in the world for the manifestation of signs and wonders, for the manifestation of the mighty power of God.

It's all right now,
It's all right now,
For Jesus is my Savior,
And it's all right now.

The great secret of everything is this: have you been *"begotten"* (1 Pet. 1:3)? If so, it is all right. It is an act within you. There are people here who are in need of a touch. The well is beside you this morning, offering life and liberty for captives. God can make this manifest. You must understand this: while faith is a great assurance and takes in God's bountiful provision, unbelief is sin. You have to see the contrast.

I am positive that there is the possibility of divine life coming to dwell within human life, but there first has to be a death. From my real knowledge of truth, I can tell you that it is the depth of death—that is, association with Jesus—that brings life. With Jesus, it was a real death. He asked His disciples, *"Are you able to drink the cup that I am about to drink, and be baptized with the baptism that I am baptized with?"* (Matt. 20:22). And they said, *"We are able"* (v. 22). He replied, *"You will indeed drink My cup, and be baptized with the baptism that I am baptized with"* (v. 23). The cup and the baptism perfectly join together. "You" cannot live if you want to bring everything into life; it is only His life that brings forth manifestations of His power. It is not within the human capacity; it is foreign to the human. The human must decrease if the power of the life of God is to be made manifest by His Spirit.

There is not room for two lives in one body. Death to self is the way for the life of the Christ of God to be manifested through you. Your human desires— human supremacy, wanting to be someone, wanting to do something special—are a tremendous hindrance and curse to your life. Not until you cease can God increase. Unbelief would then be foreign to your spiritual nature, for you would then say, *"I live by the faith of the Son of God"* (Gal. 2:20 KJV).

The Holy Spirit is the only One who can reveal Jesus, and the revelation He gives makes Jesus so real. I want to prove to you that this Word is so effective that we think it, we speak it, we act on it, and we live it. Do you find Him everywhere—in the streets, at home? Are you occupied with thinking and speaking in the Holy Spirit, praying and singing in the Holy Spirit? It is the most wonderful thing in life. It is wonderful how God works along these lines. Character is what is within you. Realize the importance of that truth; it will be helpful for all time. Paul said, *"When I am weak, then I am strong"* (2 Cor. 12:10), and, *"Who is weak, and I am not weak?"* (2 Cor. 11:29). The measure to which you are weak is the measure of your strength.

FAITH, KNOWLEDGE, SUPREMACY

When you have nothing, you can possess all things. (See 2 Corinthians 6:10.) If you rely on anything other than God, you cannot possess the greater things. The infinite God is behind the person who has no trust in earthly things; he is in a place where he is trusting in nothing but God. I have never yet condemned anyone for using methods and resources in their Christian lives and ministries, but I see the difference between having a whole Bible, a rich inheritance in God, and only a part. I see that the plan of God is so much greater than everything else. If I have Him, I have life in me; I have an abundance of this life.

Jesus walked in the knowledge that He had supreme authority and power in the Father. He was living so completely in the knowledge of the fullness of God in Him that when He met people, they were bound to believe that He was in the place where He was in the supremacy. It is wonderful that God the Holy Spirit can take us to where we know we have the supremacy in the power of the name of Jesus. This is a great truth: at every moment, you are so safe that you receive nothing less than the divine life of Him who has *"all power"* (Matt. 28:18 KJV).

I am saved by the living Word, which is Christ. Christ is the living *"substance"* (Heb. 11:1) within me. As everything was subject to Him, everything really must be subject to me, because I know that He has manifested His divine authority within me.

How can I know this? On the authority of the Word. Now, what are we to do? Jesus tells us to believe (Mark 11:23). God wants to bring us to the place of believing. He intends us to know this truth: *"He will have whatever he says"* (v. 23). On the authority of the Word of God, let me prove it.

A MAN WITH CANCER HEALED

There was a certain man who was very weak and frail in every way; his eyes were sunken, his cheekbones were sticking out, and his neck was shrunken. He came to me and said, "Can you help me?"

Could I help him? You will find that there is not a person in this place who cannot be helped. Whatever you are suffering from can be cured, and your pain can cease. If there are any persons suffering, they may be healed at once; when God is manifesting His power, there must be signs and wonders. This man told me that he had cancer, and that the physician, in removing some of the cancerous matter, had taken away his ability to swallow, and now he could not swallow. When he spoke to me, he spoke only in something like a whisper.

He pulled out a tubing, and showed me a piece about nine inches long. This left an opening in his stomach, through which he had been feeding himself with liquid for three months. He was a living skeleton, but I could help him according to the Word of God. If a person *"does not doubt in his heart, but believes that those things he says will be done, he will have whatever he says"* (v. 23). In the name of the Lord, I said to him, "Go home and eat a good supper." He went home and told his wife that the preacher said he had to have a good supper. She prepared a supper, and when it was ready, he began chewing his food over and over. But the Word of God must come to pass. I said he should have a good supper, and he was able to swallow his food; he ate until he was full, and he went to bed full. He had a new experience; life had come. But this joy was not all that he would experience. When he awoke the next morning, knowing what had happened, out of curiosity, he looked down at his stomach, and he found that God had healed him; the opening in his stomach had been closed.

All this is divine revelation. We must not measure ourselves by ourselves. If we do, we will always be small. Measure yourself by the Word of God, the great measurement that God brings to you. Don't be fearful; He wants to make us strong, powerful, stalwart, resolute, resting upon the authority of God. I can only speak along these lines, and shall we not *"be brave"* (1 Cor. 16:13)? We are those who have seen the King. We have been made alive from the dead. God has worked special miracles in us all; we have been made with one great design and purpose.

LIVING ON THE WORD

This healing was according to the Word of God. I must live on nothing else than the Word—it must mean more than my food, more than my associations, to live in this holy Word. I have been preaching faith, and I want you who are suffering from bodily pain to stand. I must deal with someone who is conspicuous. I must deal with you according to the Word of God. No one here will be overlooked. We have come here for the purpose of meeting your need; nobody will be overlooked.

Only believe, only believe,
All things are possible, only believe.

The Compassion of Faith

eloved, I believe that God would be pleased for me to read to you a passage from the fifth chapter of Mark's gospel. This is a wonderful passage; in fact, all of God's Word is wonderful. It is the Word of Life, and it is the impartation of the life of the Savior.

Now when Jesus had crossed over again by boat to the other side, a great multitude gathered to Him; and He was by the sea. And behold, one of the rulers of the synagogue came, Jairus by name. And when he saw Him, he fell at His feet and begged Him earnestly, saying, "My little daughter lies at the point of death. Come and lay Your hands on her, that she may be healed, and she will live." So Jesus went with him, and a great multitude followed Him and thronged Him. Now a certain woman had a flow of blood for twelve years, and had suffered many things from many physicians. She had spent all that she had and was no better, but rather grew worse. When she heard about Jesus, she came behind Him in the crowd and touched His garment. For she said, "If only I may touch His clothes, I shall be made well." Immediately the fountain of her blood was dried up, and she felt in her body that she was healed of the affliction. And Jesus, immediately knowing in Himself that power had gone out of Him, turned around in the crowd and said, "Who touched My clothes?" But His disciples said to Him, "You see the multitude thronging You, and You say, 'Who touched Me?'" And He looked around to see her who had done this thing. But the woman, fearing and trembling, knowing what had happened to her, came and fell down before Him and told Him the whole truth. And He said to her, "Daughter, your faith has made you well. Go in peace, and be healed of your affliction." While He was still speaking, some came from the ruler of the synagogue's house who said, "Your daughter is dead. Why trouble the Teacher any further?" As soon as Jesus heard the word that was spoken, He said to the ruler of the synagogue, "Do not be afraid; only believe." And He permitted no one to follow Him except Peter, James, and John the brother of James. Then He came to the house of the ruler of the synagogue, and saw a tumult and those who wept and wailed loudly. When He came in, He said to them, "Why make this commotion and weep? The child is not dead, but sleeping." And they ridiculed Him. But when He had put them all outside, He took the father and the mother of the child, and those who were with Him, and entered where the child was lying. Then He took

*the child by the hand, and said to her, "Talitha,
cumi," which is translated, "Little girl, I say
to you, arise." Immediately the girl arose and
walked, for she was twelve years of age. And
they were overcome with great amazement. But
He commanded them strictly that no one should
know it, and said that something should be
given her to eat.* (Mark 5:21–43)

Jesus came to give eternal life, and He also came
to make our bodies whole. I believe that God, the
Holy Spirit, wants to reveal the fullness of redemption through the power of Christ's atonement on Calvary until every soul receives a new sight of Jesus, the
Lamb of God. He is lovely. *"He is altogether lovely"*
(Song 5:16). Oh, He is so beautiful! You talk about
being arrayed with the rarest garments, but oh, Jesus
could *"weep with those who weep"* (Rom. 12:15). He
could have compassion on all. (See, for example, Matthew 9:36.) There were none in need whom He did not
see.

When Jesus was at the pool of Bethesda, He knew
all about the sick man who lay there, and understood
his situation altogether. (See John 5:2–9.) Yes, and
when He was at Nain, the compassion of the Master
was so manifested that it was victorious over death.
(See Luke 7:11–15.) Do you know that love and compassion are stronger than death? If we touch God, the
Holy Spirit, He is the ideal principle of divine life for
weaknesses. He is health. He is joy.

God wants us to know that He is waiting to
impart life. Oh, if you would only believe! You do not
need to wait another moment. Right now, as I preach,
receive the impartation of life by the power of the
Word. Do you not know that the Holy Spirit is the

breath of heaven, the breath of God, the divine impartation of power that moves in the human, raises from the dead, and makes all things alive?

One of the things that happened on the Day of Pentecost in the manifestation of the Spirit was a *"rushing mighty wind"* (Acts 2:2). The third person of the Trinity was manifested in wind, power, might, revelation, glory, and emancipation. Glory to God! I am preaching here today because of this holy, divine Person who is breath, life, revelation. His power moved me, transformed me, sent me, and revised my entire position. This *"wind"* in Acts 2:2 was the life of God coming and filling the whole place where Jesus' followers were sitting. Therefore, when I say to you, "Breathe in," I do not mean to merely breathe; I mean to breathe in God's life, God's power, the personality of God. Hallelujah!

The Scripture passage from Mark 5 that we read earlier tells of a father and mother who are in great trouble. Imagine what they are facing. They have a little daughter who is lying at the point of death. Everything else has failed, but they know that if they can find Jesus, she will be made whole. Is it possible to seek Jesus and not find Him? Never! There is not one person in this place who has truly sought Jesus and not found Him. As you seek, you will find; as you knock, the door will swing open; as you ask, you will receive (Matt. 7:7). Yes, if they can find Jesus, they know their little daughter will live.

As the father walks along the road, he notices a great commotion. He sees the dust rising a long time before he reaches the great company of people who surround Jesus. Imagine the children's voices and the people shouting. All are delighted because Jesus is in their company. Oh, this camp meeting will rise to a tremendous pitch as we look for Jesus.

Yes, the father of this little girl met Jesus; glory to God! He *"begged Him earnestly, saying, 'My little daughter lies at the point of death. Come and lay Your hands on her, that she may be healed, and she will live.' So Jesus went with him"* (Mark 5:23–24). I want you to know that this same Jesus is in the midst of His people today. He is right here with His ministry of power and blessing.

Now, as Jesus went with the man, something happened. *"A certain woman [who] had a flow of blood for twelve years...came behind Him in the crowd and touched His garment"* (vv. 25, 27). This poor woman was in an awful state. She had spent all her money on physicians and *"was no better, but rather grew worse"* (v. 26). This poor woman said, *"If only I may touch His clothes, I shall be made well"* (v. 28). No doubt, she thought of her weakness, but faith is never weak. She may have been very weary, but faith is never weary. The opportunity came for her to touch Him, and *"immediately the fountain of her blood was dried up, and she felt in her body that she was healed of the affliction"* (v. 29).

The opportunity comes to you now to be healed. Will you believe? Will you touch Him? There is something in a living faith that is different from anything else. I have seen marvelous things accomplished just because people have said, "Lord, I believe."

Jesus knew that power had gone out of Him, and He said, *"Who touched My clothes?"* (v. 30). The woman was fearful and trembling, but she

> *fell down before Him and told Him the whole truth. And He said to her, "Daughter, your faith has made you well. Go in peace, and be healed of your affliction." While He was still*

speaking, some came from the ruler of the syn-
agogue's house who said, "Your daughter is
dead. Why trouble the Teacher any further?"
                                    (Mark 5:33–35)

But Jesus encouraged the ruler of the synagogue, and said, *"Do not be afraid; only believe"* (v. 36). When He reached the ruler's house,

He took the child by the hand, and said to her,
"Talitha, cumi," which is translated, "Little
girl, I say to you, arise." Immediately the girl
arose and walked, for she was twelve years of
age. And they were overcome with great amaze-
ment.   (Mark 5:41–42)

Ah, what things God does for us when we only believe! He is *"rich to all who call upon Him"* (Rom. 10:12). What possibilities there are in this meeting—if we would only believe in the divine presence, for God is here. The power of the Spirit is here. How many of you dare to rise and claim your healing? Who will dare to rise and claim his rights of perfect health? *"All things are possible to him who believes"* (Mark 9:23). Jesus is the living *"substance"* of faith. (See Hebrews 11:1.) You can be made perfectly whole by the blood of Jesus. We must believe in the revelation of the Spirit's power, and see our blessed position in the risen Christ.

> Only believe! Only believe!
> All things are possible, only believe!

Overcoming the World

I think it will please God if I read to you the fifth chapter of the first epistle of John. It contains one of those wonderful and divine truths of God that brings the love of God into our lives, and this verifies, in every situation of life, that we are of God. There is an essential truth in this chapter that will give us a clear discernment of our position in Christ.

Whoever believes that Jesus is the Christ is born of God, and everyone who loves Him who begot also loves him who is begotten of Him. By this we know that we love the children of God, when we love God and keep His commandments. For this is the love of God, that we keep His commandments. And His commandments are not burdensome. For whatever is born of God overcomes the world. And this is the victory that has overcome the world; our faith. Who is he who overcomes the world, but he who believes that Jesus is the Son of God? This is He who came by water and blood; Jesus Christ; not only by water, but by water and blood. And it is the Spirit who bears witness, because the Spirit is truth. For there are three that bear witness in heaven: the Father, the Word, and the Holy Spirit; and these three are one. And there are three that bear witness on earth: the Spirit, the water, and the blood; and these three agree as one. If we receive the witness of men, the witness of God is greater; for this is the witness of God which He has testified of His Son. He who believes in the Son of God has the witness in himself; he who does not believe God has made Him a liar, because he has not believed the testimony that God has given of His Son. And this is the testimony: that God has given us eternal life, and this life is in His Son. He who has the Son has life; he who does not have the Son of God does not have life. These things I have written to you who believe in the name of the Son of God, that you may know that you have eternal life, and that you may continue to believe in the name of the Son of God. Now this is the confidence that we have in Him, that if we ask anything according to His will, He hears us. And if we know that He hears us, whatever we ask, we know that we have the petitions that we have asked of Him. If anyone sees his brother sinning a sin which does not lead to death, he will ask, and He will give him life for those who commit sin not leading to death. There is sin leading to death. I do not say that he should pray about that. All unrighteousness is sin, and there is sin not leading to death. We know that whoever is born of God does not sin; but he who has been born of God keeps himself, and the wicked one does not touch him. We know that we are of God, and the whole world lies under the sway of the wicked one. And we know that the Son of God has come and has given us an understanding, that we may know Him who is true; and we are in Him who is true, in His Son Jesus Christ. This is the true God and eternal life. Little children, keep yourselves from idols. Amen.

God wants us all to be so built up in truth, righteousness, and the life of God that every person we come in contact with may truly know that we are of God. And we who are of God can *"assure our hearts before Him"* (1 John 3:19), and we can have perfect *"confidence toward God"* (v. 21).

THE LIVING WORD

There is something more in the believer than words. Words are of little effect unless they have a personal manifestation of God. We must not look at the Word as only a written Word. The Word is a living fact that works living truths in the human body—changing it, moving it, until a person is a living fact of God's inheritance, until God is reigning in his body, reigning in the world and over it. In conversation or activity, the person is a production of God. It is truly a human plan first, but it is covered with God's inheritance.

I now want to come to the Word itself, and, by the grace of God, to bring us into a place where it will be impossible, whatever happens, to move us from our plan. Let us look at the first verse: *"Whoever believes that Jesus is the Christ is born of God, and everyone who loves Him who begot also loves him who is begotten of Him* (1 John 5:1).

There are hundreds of so-called religions everywhere. But look! All these differences of opinions will wither away, and there will be a perfect oneness and divine union of belief in Christ, and it will surely have to come to pass. You ask, "How is this possible?" The Bible is truth; it is the Word of God; it is God Himself portrayed in Word. You see God in the Word. God can manifest Himself through that Word until we become a living factor of that truth because *"God is light and in Him is no darkness"* (1 John 1:5). God is life. God is revelation. God is manifestation. God is operation. So God wants to truly bring us into a place where we have the clearest revelation—even though there may be much conviction through it—the clearest revelation of where we stand.

WHAT IT MEANS TO HAVE THE NEW BIRTH

"Whoever believes that Jesus is the Christ is born of God" (1 John 5:1). What is the outcome of being born of God? It is God's life, God's truth, God's walk. It is communion, fellowship, oneness, and like-mindedness with God. All that pertains to holiness, righteousness, and truth comes forth out of this new birth unto righteousness. And in it, through it, and by it we are in a perfect, regenerated position, even as we have come into light through it.

Again, it is an impartation of love, and an expression of Himself, for *"God is love"* (1 John 4:8, 16). The first breathing or revelation of light of the new creation within the soul is so pure, so unadulterated, so perfect, and so righteous that, if you go back to when you were first enlightened and had the

76

revelation, when you first believed in your heart, you will remember that you felt so holy, that you had so much love, that you were in a paradise of wonderment. You had no desire for sin; sin had lost its appeal.

There you were with a new birth unto righteousness, filled with the first love of purity and truth. You felt as if everybody was going to be saved, and that the world was going to be turned upside down, because you had received the new birth. That was the first touch. It was a remarkable revelation to me when I first saw that God had purposed that every newborn babe in Christ is called to be a saint (Rom. 1:7; 1 Cor. 1:2); called *"from darkness to light"* (Acts 26:18; see 1 Peter 2:9), *"from the power of Satan to God"* (Acts 26:18)—separated to God at the revelation that Jesus is the Son of God.

Another result of the new birth, which I just mentioned, was that for days and days something so remarkable came over your life that you neither had a desire to sin nor did sin. How many have a recollection of those moments? Praise God! God had designed the plan for you before the world began (2 Tim. 1:9). I believe that God wants to open your heart and mind to why you are here, to a purpose of being that He predestined for you.

We need to be so established with facts that there won't be anything in the world that is able to move us from our perfect position. How many people are there who, though sin is striving with them, though evil forces are around them, still never remember a day when God did not also strive with them, drawing them back to Him? It is impossible to be in the world without satanic forces trying to bid very loudly for our lives, but how many are there who, from their very infancy, have always remembered that the good hand of God was with them? If you knew the Scriptures, you could say, like Paul, that, from your mother's womb, God had called you (Gal. 1:15–16).

GOD HAS GREAT PURPOSES FOR US

Beloved, God has predestined us. Two great truths in the Scriptures are these: *"He who believes in Him is not condemned,"* and *"He who does not believe is condemned already"* (John 3:18). God has covered the world with the blood of Jesus, and every man has the offer of redemption through Christ, whether he will receive it or not. (See 1 John 2:2; Col. 1:19–23.) But there are some people whom God has wonderfully chosen *"before the foundation of the world"* (Eph. 1:4). And as surely as we are alive, we can say that God has predestined us, even to this day. Although you have had times of defeat, the tendency, the longings, the cries, and the desires of your whole life have been that you have wanted God.

See how much God has for you in the Word! God wants people who are mighty in the Spirit, who are full of power. God has no such thing as small measures for man. God has great purposes for man. God has determined, by His power and His grace, through the Son, to bring *"many sons to glory"* (Heb. 2:10), clothed with the Holy One from heaven.

Interpretation of Tongues
The Lord of life and glory, who has "begotten us to a living hope," has "chosen us before the foundation of the world" so that He may manifest His Son in us, and get the glory over the

powers of darkness and the Devil and every evil
thing, so that we may reign over the powers of
the Devil.

The Holy Spirit is jealous over us. How He longs
for us to catch the breath of His Spirit! How He longs
for us to be moved in union with Himself, so that
He could breathe any thought from heaven through
the natural, and thereby chasten the natural by His
divine plan, so that you would have a new faith or a
revelation of God. You would be so perfect before Him
that there would not be a thing that Satan could say
contrary to God's child.

Hear what Satan said to God about Job: *"Have
You not made a hedge around him?"* (Job 1:10). God
said, *"All that he has is in your power; only do not lay
a hand on his person"* (Job 1:12). We see that God put
a hedge around His child. Oh, that we would believe!
Listen to what Jesus said:

> *Do you not yet understand, or remember the
> five loaves of the five thousand and how many
> baskets you took up? Nor the seven loaves of
> the four thousand and how many large baskets
> you took up? How is it you do not understand?*
> (Matt. 16:9–11)

Oh, if we only had not forgotten the blessings and
the *"pressed down"* measures (Luke 6:38), everything
would be moved by the manifestation of the children
of God, who would stand by the power of the righteousness of heaven and move the world.

*"Who is he who overcomes the world, but he who
believes that Jesus is the Son of God?"* (1 John 5:5).
That is a very beautiful truth! *"For whatever is born*

of God overcomes the world. And this is the victory that has overcome the world; our faith" (v. 4). We will have to come into divine measurement, divine revelation. The possibilities are ours.

BELIEVING AND RECEIVING

One day, I was in Belfast, Ireland. I had a friend there named Morris. He had been with us at my hometown of Bradford, England, and I wanted to see him, so I went to his house and said, "Is Brother Morris here?" The woman there answered, "It is not Morris you want. God sent you for me. I am a brokenhearted woman. I am going through death, having the greatest trial of my life. Come in." I went in, and she continued, "My husband is a deacon in the Presbyterian Church, and you know that when you were here, God filled me with the Holy Spirit. As a deacon's wife, I sat in a prominent place in the church. The Spirit of the Lord came upon me, and I was so filled with joy that I broke out in tongues. The whole church turned around to look at me for making such a disturbance."

At the close of the meeting, the deacons and the pastor came to her husband, saying, "You cannot be a deacon in this church because of your wife's behavior." It nearly broke his heart. When he saw that he was going to lose all his influence, he came home in bitterness. He and his wife had lived together for many years and had never known a disagreement. After causing much trouble, he left his wife with the words, "I will never come near you again as long as I live."

After she told me the story, we prayed, and the power of God shook her. God showed me that He would give to her all she required. "Madam, wake up!" I exclaimed. "Look, the situation is yours. God has given you the situation. It is according to the Word of God: *'For the unbelieving husband is sanctified by the wife, and the unbelieving wife is sanctified by the husband....For how do you know, O wife, whether you will save your husband? Or how do you know, O husband, whether you will save your wife?'* (1 Cor. 7:14, 16). You will be the means of your husband's being saved and baptized." "Yes," she replied, "if I could believe he would ever come back, but he will never come back."

"Look," I said, "the Word of God says, *'If two of you agree on earth concerning anything that they ask, it will be done for them by My Father in heaven'* (Matt. 18:19). We will agree that he will come home tonight."

Interpretation of Tongues

God has designed a purpose for His people. And the word of truth comes to us by interpretation: "Whatever you bind on earth will be bound in heaven. And whatever you loose on earth will be loosed in heaven."

I advised her, "When he comes home, show him that you love him. It is possible that he won't accept your love. As soon as he goes to bed, you get down before God and get filled, just as you were here. Then touch him in God."

Her husband was obliged to come home. If you believe God, whatever you desire comes to pass. He marched up and down in the house as though he never saw her, and then he retired to his room. Then she got down before God. Oh, the place of all places where God comes to the soul! The Spirit came upon her until her whole being was filled with the flame of heaven.

Then she touched him. He screamed, rolled off onto the floor, and cried for mercy. She never left him until he was filled with the Holy Spirit.

Nothing happens to the believer except what is good for him. *"All things work together for good to those who love God"* (Rom. 8:28). But we must not forget this additional injunction, *"To those who are the called according to His purpose"* (v. 28). Remember, you are called *"according to His purpose"* in the working out of the power of God within you for the salvation of others. God has you for a purpose.

BEING A CHILD OF GOD

Look, beloved, *"I want you to be without care"* (1 Cor. 7:32). How many people are bound and helpless and have no testimony because of their anxiety! Hear what the Scripture says: *"You have hidden these things from the wise and prudent and have revealed them to babes. Even so, Father, for so it seemed good in Your sight"* (Matt. 11:25–26). We have to become trusting children of our heavenly Father.

The first thing that God truly does with a newborn child of God is to keep him as a child. There are wonderful things for children. The difference between a child and the *"wise and prudent"* is this: the wise man knows too much, and the prudent man is too careful. But babies are different! They eagerly receive. When our children were babies, they were sometimes so ravenous that we had to pull the bottle back from them, lest they swallow the bottle with the milk! A child cannot dress himself, but needs his parents to dress him. In a similar way, God clothes His children. He has a special garment for His children, white and beautiful. God says there is no spot on His children

(Eph. 5:27), telling them, "You are pure, *'altogether lovely'* (Song 5:16)." A baby cannot talk. Likewise, it is lovely for the child of God to know that he does not have to think about what he will say, that the Holy Spirit will speak through him. (See Matthew 10:19–20.) If you are a child, if you give everything over to God, He can speak through you. He loves His children. Oh, how beautifully He sees to His children! How kind and good He is!

Overcoming through Belief in Jesus

"Who is he who overcomes the world, but he who believes that Jesus is the Son of God?" (1 John 5:5). That pure, that holy, that devoted Person who made the world submits His will to Almighty God, and God uses His will and dwells in Him in fullness. He meets the world's need. He comes in at the dry time when there is no wine, and He makes the wine. (See John 2:1–10.) Glory to God. When there is no bread, He comes and makes the bread. (See, for example, Matthew 14:15–21.)

He who believes that Jesus is the Son of God overcomes the world (1 John 5:5). You may ask, "How can a person overcome the world just because he believes that Jesus is the Son of God?" It is because Jesus is so holy, and you become His *"habitation"* (Eph. 2:22 KJV). Jesus is so sweet; His love surpasses all understanding. His wisdom surpasses all knowledge (Rom. 11:33); therefore, He comes to you with the wisdom of God and not the wisdom of this world. (See 1 Corinthians 2:6–7.) He comes to you with peace, but not as this world gives (John 14:27). He comes to you with boundless blessing, with a measure *"pressed down... and running over"* (Luke 6:38). You do not require the world, for you have food to eat that the world does not know of. (See John 4:32.) God is a *"rewarder of those who diligently seek Him"* (Heb. 11:6), for those who seek Him *"shall not lack any good thing"* (Ps. 34:10).

Beloved, where are your boundaries? There are heights and depths and lengths and breadths to the love of God (Eph. 3:17–19). The Word of God contains the principles of life. "I" no longer live, but Another mightier than I lives (Gal. 2:20). My desires have gone into the desires of God. This is lovely! This life is so perfected in the Holy Spirit that God is continually bringing forth *"things new and old"* (Matt. 13:52).

"Who is he who overcomes the world, but he who believes that Jesus is the Son of God?" (1 John 5:5). How do we overcome? We come into this great inheritance of the Spirit. We make it our earnest desire that there will not be anything in us that Satan could use in overcoming us. Remember the words of Jesus, *"The ruler of this world is coming, and he has nothing in Me"* (John 14:30). We desire to reach such a place as this. Is it possible? Brothers and sisters, it is the design of the Master. Without holiness, no one will see the Lord (Heb. 12:14). *"He who has been born of God keeps himself, and the wicked one does not touch him"* (1 John 5:18).

Surely the Lord is not going to send you away empty. He wants to satisfy your longing soul with good things. *"Whatever is born of God overcomes the world. And this is the victory that has overcome the world; our faith"* (v. 4).

THREE KINDS OF FAITH

Let me speak about three kinds of faith. There is a good, there is a better, and there is a best. God has the best. In this Pentecostal outpouring, I find that some people are satisfied with "tongues." That would never satisfy me. I want the Person who gives them. I am the hungriest man that you have ever seen. I want all He has. Unless God gives to me, I am a perfectly spoiled baby. "Father," I say, "You will have to give to me."

When I was a little boy, I would go to my father and say, "Father, will you give me some birdlime?" "No, no," he would answer. I knew just what he meant from the way he said it. I would plead, "Father, father, father, father." I would follow him as he walked out. "Father, father, father." Mother would ask, "Why don't you give the lad what he wants?'"

I got to the place where I believed my father liked to hear me say his name. If you only knew how God likes to hear us say, "Father, my Father!" Oh, how He loves His children! I will never forget when my wife and I had our first baby. He was asleep in the cradle. We both went to him, and my wife said, "I cannot bear to have him sleep any longer. I want him!" And I remember waking the baby because she wanted him. *"If you then, being evil, know how to give good gifts to your children, how much more will your heavenly Father give the Holy Spirit to those who ask Him!"* (Luke 11:13). Ah, He is such a lovely Father!

"But," you say, "sometimes I give in to temptation." Never mind; I am going to bring you to a point where you never need to give in. Praise God! If I did not know the almighty power of God, I would jump off this platform. Because we are quickened, made alive, we move into the new spirit, the spirit of fellowship with God that was lost in the Garden of Eden. Oh, hallelujah; new birth, new life, new person!

Human faith works, and then waits for its wages. That is not saving faith. Then there is the gift of faith. *"For by grace you have been saved through faith, and that not of yourselves; it is the gift of God"* (Eph. 2:8). Faith is what God gave you in order to believe. *"Whoever believes that Jesus is the Christ is born of God"* (1 John 5:1). The sacrifice of redemption is complete, and God has kept you because you could not keep yourself (John 17:12; 1 Pet. 1:3–5).

I want to tell you of something that does not fail. Let us read Acts 26:16–18. The Lord Jesus said to Saul,

> *But rise and stand on your feet; for I have appeared to you for this purpose, to make you a minister and a witness both of the things which you have seen and of the things which I will yet reveal to you. I will deliver you from the Jewish people, as well as from the Gentiles, to whom I now send you, to open their eyes, in order to turn them from darkness to light, and from the power of Satan to God, that they may receive forgiveness of sins and an inheritance among those who are sanctified by faith in Me.*

That is faith from God, saving faith—not human faith. In 1 Corinthians 12:9, we read, *"To another* [is given] *faith by the same Spirit."* When my faith fails, then another faith lays hold of me.

AN INSANE WOMAN HEALED THROUGH FAITH

One day, I called at a home where a woman had not slept for seven weeks. She was rolling from one side of the bed to the other. In came a young man with a baby in his arms. He stooped down over the mother to try to kiss her. Instantly she rolled to the other side of the bed. Going around to her, the young man touched the lips of the mother with the baby, in order to try to bring her to consciousness again. But she switched to the other side. I could see that the young man was brokenhearted.

"What have you done for this woman?" I asked. "Everything," they replied. "We have had doctors here, we have injected morphine, and so forth." The sister said, "We must put her in an asylum. I am tired and worn out." I asked, "Have you tried God?" The husband answered, "Do you think we believe in God here? We have no confidence in anything. If you call anything like this God, we have no fellowship with it."

Oh, I was done, then! A young woman grinned in my face and slammed the door. The compassion in me was so moved that I did not know what to do. I began to cry, and my faith lifted me right up. Thank God for faith that lifted. I felt Another *"like the Son of God"* (Heb. 7:3) grip me. The Spirit of the Lord came upon me, and I said, "In the name of Jesus, come out of her!" She fell asleep and did not awaken for fourteen hours. She awakened perfectly sane. Beloved, there is a place in which we know the Son of God that absolutely overcomes the world.

At one time, I thought that I had the Holy Spirit. Now I know that the Holy Spirit has me. There is a difference between our hanging onto God and God lifting us up. There is a difference between my having a desire and God's desire filling my soul. There is a difference between natural compassion and the compassion of Jesus, which never fails. Human faith fails, but the faith of Jesus never fails.

Oh, beloved, I see a new dawning through these glorious truths: assemblies loving one another, being all of one accord. Until that time comes, there will be deficiencies. Hear what the Scripture says: *"Everyone who loves Him who begot also loves him who is begotten of Him"* (1 John 5:1), and *"By this all will know that you are My disciples, if you have love for one another"* (John 13:35). Love is the secret and center of the divine position. Build upon God.

You may be asking, "What is the gift of faith?" It is where God moves you to pray. In the Bible, we read about a man named Elijah who had *"a nature like ours"* (James 5:17). The sins of the people were grieving the heart of God, and the whole house of Ahab was in an evil state. But God moved upon Elijah and gave him an inward cry, and he said, *"There shall not be dew nor rain these years, except at my word"* (1 Kings 17:1). The result was that *"it did not rain on the land for three years and six months"* (James 5:17). Oh, if we only dared to believe God! *"A man with a nature like ours"* (v. 17) was stirred with almightiness! *"And he prayed again, and the heaven gave rain, and the earth produced its fruit"* (v. 18).

Brother, sister, you are now in the robing room. God is giving you another day to come into line, for you to lay aside everything that has hindered you, for you to forget the past. And I ask you, How many of you want to receive from God a faith that cannot be denied? I have learned that if I dare to lift up my hands in faith, God will fill them. Come on, beloved, seek God, and let us get a real touch of heaven. God is moving.

This day is the beginning of days, a day when the Lord will not forsake His own but will meet us. Come near to God! Jesus, Jesus, bless us! We are so needy,

Lord. Jesus, my Lord! Oh, Jesus, Jesus, Jesus! Oh, my Savior, my Savior! Oh, such love! Mighty God! Oh, loving Master! Blessed, blessed Jesus! There is none like Jesus! There is none as good as He! There is none as sweet as He! Oh, blessed Christ of reality, come! Hallelujah!

"The Secret Place"

*He who dwells in the secret place of the Most High
shall abide under the shadow of the Almighty. I will
say of the LORD, "He is my refuge and my fortress;
my God, in Him I will trust." Surely He shall deliver
you from the snare of the fowler and from the perilous
pestilence. He shall cover you with His feathers, and
under His wings you shall take refuge; His truth shall
be your shield and buckler. You shall not be afraid of
the terror by night, nor of the arrow that flies by day,
nor of the pestilence that walks in darkness, nor of the
destruction that lays waste at noonday. A thousand
may fall at your side, and ten thousand at your right
hand; but it shall not come near you. Only with
your eyes shall you look, and see the reward of the
wicked. Because you have made the LORD, who is my
refuge, even the Most High, your dwelling place, no
evil shall befall you, nor shall any plague come near
your dwelling; for He shall give His angels charge
over you, to keep you in all your ways. In their hands
they shall bear you up, lest you dash your foot against
a stone. You shall tread upon the lion and the cobra,*

the young lion and the serpent you shall trample underfoot. "Because he has set his love upon Me, therefore I will deliver him; I will set him on high, because he has known My name. He shall call upon Me, and I will answer him; I will be with him in trouble; I will deliver him and honor him. With long life I will satisfy him, and show him My salvation."
—Psalm 91

The *"crown of life"* (James 1:12; Rev. 2:10–11) is for the overcomer; it is not for those *"at ease* [smug] *in Zion"* (Amos 6:1). We must be in the place where God can depend on us, never giving in, knowing no defeat, always making our stand by a living faith and gaining the victory. Faith is the victory. *"This is the work of God, that you believe in Him whom He sent"* (John 6:29).

England once had a war with France. The French took some prisoners, among them a drummer boy. Napoleon ordered him to sound a retreat, but he said no, he had never learned one! God never wants you to retreat in the face of the Enemy, but to learn the victory song, and to overcome. Praise the Lord. There are two kinds of shouts: a shout that is made and a shout that makes you. There are men of God, but many men are God's men. There is a place where you take hold of God, but there is a better place where God takes hold of you. *"He who dwells in the secret place of the Most High shall abide under the shadow of the Almighty."*

Do you know the presence of the Almighty? It is wonderful; it is a surety. There is no wavering, no unbelief there. There is no unrest there; it is perfect.

My great desire is to see believers *"strong in the Lord"* (Eph. 6:10) by dwelling in *"the secret place"* that is known to all who fear Him. There are two kinds of fear of God: one is to have a reverential awe of Him, and the other is to be afraid of Him. I hope none of you are afraid of God. Unbelievers are afraid of God, but believers may have a fear of God, a reverence for Him, in which they would rather die than grieve Him. They may have peace, power, and fellowship with God.

This is the will of God for all; it is His will for the world. No price is too great to pay to enter into this peace, power, and fellowship. It is our inheritance; Christ purchased it. It is the covering of the presence of the Almighty. What a covering the unfolding of His will is! *"The secret of the LORD is with those who fear Him"* (Ps. 25:14).

THE PRESENCE OF THE ALMIGHTY

Moses knew something about the presence of the Almighty: *"If Your Presence does not go with us, do not bring us up from here"* (Exod. 33:15). *"[Those] who [dwell] in the secret place."* What does being in God's presence do? It dares me to believe all that God says; it assists me in laying hold of the promises. God so indwells us that we become a force, a power, of God's abiding, until *"death is swallowed up in victory"* (1 Cor. 15:54).

We have a great salvation, filled with inspiration, with no limitation, making known the wonders of God. Psalm 91:2 says, *"I will say of the LORD, 'He is my refuge and my fortress; my God, in Him I will trust.'"* If you are dwelling *"in the secret place of the Most High,"* as it says in verse one, then you will experience what it says in verse two—a substance of faith, the fact of God's presence worked out in your lives. You must have an inward fact. You are always beyond argument when you deal in facts. We must have facts, not fears or feelings.

"*I will say of the* LORD, *'He is my refuge.'*" Who will say this? He who abides. There is no complaining there, no bad temper, no irritability; all is swept away when we dwell in the presence of the Almighty, the covering of God.

Even the best of humanity is not good (Isa. 64:6; Rom. 7:18). Jesus was manifested to "*destroy the works of the devil*" (1 John 3:8).

> *For what the law could not do in that it was weak through the flesh, God did by sending His own Son in the likeness of sinful flesh, on account of sin: He condemned sin in the flesh.*
> (Rom. 8:3)

God sent forth Jesus "*in the likeness of sinful flesh,*" in the mightiness of His power; and, in the midst of flesh, He condemned it. "*The law of the Spirit of life*" (v. 2) destroys all that must be destroyed. When we are "*dead indeed to sin, but alive to God*" (Rom. 6:11), then we are above everything in Him, "*who is above all, and through all, and in you all*" (Eph. 4:6). This existence in God is not found in our sinful human nature, nor does it grow in Eden's garden; it is the gift of God from heaven. We belong to the "*new creation*" (2 Cor. 5:17); it is a wonderful place of life. It is life that is "*free from the law of sin and death*" (Rom. 8:2). Can we remain there?

GOD WILL KEEP US IN HIMSELF

He never forgets to keep me,
He never forgets to keep me;

My Father has many dear children,
But He never forgets to keep me

Has He forgotten to keep you? No! He cannot
forget. God has much in store for you. There was a
time when the children of Israel hung their harps on
the willows when they were in captivity (see Psalm
137:1–4), and sometimes the believer does the same.
I have seen thousands of people delivered from evil
power since I last saw you. However, there is a great
weakness in the land; it is lack of knowledge. People
"[hew] *themselves cisterns; broken cisterns that can
hold no water*" (Jer. 2:13). But those who know the
Word of God have no fear. God's Word is the great
antidote to evil. "*There is no fear in love; but perfect
love casts out fear*" (1 John 4:18).

Where is God? He is in the Word. He has embodied Himself in the Word. The Word spells destruction
to all evil. He who dwells in love is the master of situations. There is no fear, no sickness, a perfect redemption. Some say, "Does it last? Does the healing hold?"
What God does, He does forever. Thirty-five years ago,
God healed me. My whole body was weak. My teeth
were decayed, but God healed them. At sixty-two, I
am as fresh as a boy. Now, Devil, take that! It is
God's plan, which is better than any other plan. The
Bible has so many precious promises, wealth beyond
all price.

Some people exchange God's plan for fear; they
abandon God's wonderful plan for a feeling! Be real,
in accordance with God's plan. The waverer gets nothing (James 1:5–6 KJV). Real faith is establishment.
How can I get it? "*Abide under the shadow of the
Almighty.*" Don't change. Remain in the presence of
God, the glory of God. Pay any price to abide under

that covering. The secret of victory is to abide where
victory abides.

> Higher, higher, nothing dreading;
> Never, never let me stop;
> In Your footsteps keep me treading;
> Give me strength to reach the top.

Interpretation of Tongues

Jesus has become the "author and the finisher
of faith." "Your life is hid with Christ in God."
There is no limitation where the Holy Breath
blows an inward cry after Him, "for with the
heart man believes unto righteousness; and
with the mouth confession is made unto salvation."

*"Because he has set his love upon Me, therefore I
will deliver him; I will set him on high, because he has
known My name."* Do you know His name? If so, *"you
will ask what you desire, and it shall be done for you"*
(John 15:7). You will have communion with Jesus,
fellowship divine; you will not whisper the name of
Jesus, but will have a knowledge of the name. *"He
shall call upon Me, and I will answer him."* Feed upon
the Word. *"With long life I will satisfy him, and show
him My salvation."* Amen.

Children of God

This is a banquet of love, where Jesus is looking upon us from heaven and making Himself known to us. It is surely the manifestation of God's love when we read in His Word, *"For as the heavens are high above the earth, so great is His mercy* [loving-kindness] *toward those who fear Him"* (Ps. 103:11). Surely, beloved, God intends to strengthen us through our coming near to Him, so that we may believe that our weaknesses will be turned into strength, and that our unbelief will be made into living faith. The dew of His presence, the power of His love, will be so active upon us that we will be changed by His wonderful Word.

I want to lift you to a place where you will dare to believe that God is waiting to bless you abundantly, beyond all that you can *"ask or think"* (Eph. 3:20).

Are you ready? "What for?" you ask. To get before God today with such living faith that you will dare to believe that all things are possible concerning you. (See Mark 9:23.)

Are you ready? What for? To know today that God's mercy never fails. Though you fail, He is still full of mercy.

Are you ready? You are? Then God will surely grant you a very rich blessing, so that you will forget all your poverty and come into a bountiful place of supply. You will never have—understand this, for God means it—you will never have any barrenness, but you will be brought into His treasures; He will cover you with His bountifulness, and you will know that the God of the Most High reigns.

What Manner of Love

The Lord has given me the privilege of bringing before you another message, which I trust will stir you all and change you in a very remarkable way.

The Lord is still leading me along the line of the gifts of the Spirit, but I want to take a little break from talking about them because we have had so much teaching on the gifts, and I now want to put you in the position where you are worthy of receiving and operating in these divine appointments with God.

To this end, let us consider 1 John 3:1–10:

Behold what manner of love the Father has bestowed on us, that we should be called children of God! Therefore the world does not know us, because it did not know Him. Beloved, now we are children of God; and it has not yet been revealed what we shall be, but we know that when He is revealed, we shall be like Him, for we shall see Him as He is. And everyone who has this hope in Him purifies himself, just as He is pure. Whoever commits sin also commits lawlessness, and sin is lawlessness. And you know that He was manifested to take away our sins, and in Him there is no sin. Whoever abides in Him does not sin. Whoever sins has neither seen Him nor known Him. Little children, let no one deceive you. He who practices righteousness is righteous, just as He is righteous. He who sins is of the devil, for the devil has sinned from the beginning. For this purpose the Son of God was manifested, that He might destroy the works of the devil. Whoever has been born of God does not sin, for His seed remains in him; and he cannot sin, because he has been born of God. In this the children of God and the children of the devil are manifest: Whoever does not practice righteousness is not of God, nor is he who does not love his brother. (1 John 3:1–10)

This passage is one of the pinnacles of truth. A pinnacle of truth is something that leads you to a place of sovereignty, of purity, a place where you cannot be moved by any situation. You have a fixed position. You take the position clearly on the authority of the Word of Jesus.

God intends to let the following truths ring through our hearts distinctly, clearly, marvelously: We are free from sin. We are children of God. We are heirs of the kingdom of His righteousness.

The opening word of 1 John 3 is one of those words in which we find stimulation: *"Behold."* (The Bible uses certain words to draw our attention to what precedes or follows. For example, in Hebrews, you will find the frequent occurrence of a word that has a lot to do with opening our understanding of the Scriptures: *"therefore."*) This beautiful word *"behold"* means, "Awake; open; listen, for God is speaking."

What is He saying? *"Behold what manner of love the Father has bestowed on us, that we should be called children of God!"* (1 John 3:1).

"What manner of love"! God's love is manifold, and much more. It is full of expression. It was God who looked past your weaknesses, your human depravities, every part of your nature and character, which you knew were absolutely out of order. He has washed you; He has cleansed you; He has beautified you; and He looks at you and says, "You are lovely! I see no spot of sin upon you; there is no spot. (See Song 4:7.) You are now my children."

Interpretation of Tongues

For the Lord is "gentle, easy to be entreated, without partiality," full of goodness and faith. He sees beyond all weakness, looks at the "Son of His love" because of the shed blood, opens unto us the treasures of His great love, and says to us, "'You are fair, my love, you are fair; I have called you into my banqueting house; I have decked you with the rarest jewels'; for you will have gifts, and the beatitudes will cover you, and my grace will follow you, and I will give you to understand the mysteries of the hidden things."

THE ORDER OF SONSHIP

"That we should be called children of God! Therefore the world does not know us, because it did not know Him" (1 John 3:1). The world does not know us in our sonship. We have to be strangers to the world's knowledge. We have to surpass all that the world knows, even as we are in the midst of the world.

I want us to examine ourselves to see if this sonship is ours, to see if we are in the order of perfect sonship. After you have confirmed this, you may strengthen yourself in God and believe for anything to come to pass. But you must examine yourself to see if you are in the Father. (See 2 Corinthians 13:5.)

The greatest blessing that will come to you will be that the Word of Life, in going forth, will create in you a deeper desire for God. If you are in the Father, as the Spirit is giving the Word, you will have a greater longing for God, for the holiness of God, for the righteousness of God; for He has to make you know today that, as He is pure, you have to be pure. (See 1 John 3:3.)

Don't stumble at the Word. If Jesus says anything, if the Word conveys anything to your mind, don't stumble at the Word. Believe that God is greater than you are, greater than your heart (1 John 3:20), greater than your mind, and can establish you in righteousness even when your thoughts and your knowledge are absolutely against it.

God blots out our transgressions in a thick cloud; and our sins, our iniquities, He will never remember. (See Isaiah 43:25.) I often find that people misunderstand God's Word because they bring only their minds to the Word, and when the Word does not exactly fit what their minds expected, they do not get liberty. They want the Word to come to their minds. It will never happen. You have to be submissive to God.

The Word of God is true. If you understand what is true and right, you can always be on the line of gaining strength, overcoming situations, living in the world but over it, making everything subject to you in Christ.

Do All to the Glory of God

One day, after I held a meeting, a man came to me and said, "Your ministry makes me feel that there is something radically wrong with me. I am a strong man, to look at; there is apparently no weakness about me. But I am ashamed of myself. I have three big lads, and they are doing the work of men, and I know it is not right. Here I am, a big man, and if I do any work for my business, I become incapacitated. I have just had three weeks of bed rest from working one day."

He had a business of carrying coal from house to house in bags that weighed 112 pounds. Every time he picked up a bag and carried it to a house, his whole frame gave way and he had to go to bed.

"Why, brother," I said, "you have never come into the line of truth. You are stranger to the truth of the Word of God."

There are any number of people who have not learned yet how they are the masters of their own bodies, masters of all kinds of work, masters of everything. You have to be a child of God in the earth—over your work, over your mind, over your body, over your life.

Interpretation of Tongues

It is God who opens the heart and gives us understanding, for unless the Spirit gives life to the world, you will still be held; but let the Spirit lift you by the Word, and you will find you will come into perfect freedom today, for God takes the Word, pours it into your heart, and opens your understanding. And you are in liberty because the Word of God makes everybody free, and "the Word of God is not bound."

From Romans 7:25, we see how we can be masters over every manual labor in God: *"So then, with the mind I myself serve the law of God, but with the flesh the law of sin."* The result of being controlled by *"the flesh"* is serving *"the law of sin."* We need to serve *"the law of God."*

"My brother," I said to the man with the coal business, "you have carried those bags of coal with your body, and you have allowed your flesh to control your body, and you have become incapacitated."

People do this all the time.

Now, what is *"the law of sin"*? Every kind of toilsome work is the result of the law of sin. Is work sin? No, it is not sin. It is what the law brought. There was no toilsome work before the Fall; it came through sin. Because of sin, you have to eat your bread by the sweat of your brow (Gen. 3:19); sweat is a symbol of sin.

The law of sin has brought sweat, disease, weakness, calamity, and all kinds of depression. Is it sin, then, to work? No, it is not sin to work.

I went to an insane asylum one day, and I said to the man there, "What is the first indication that a man has gotten back his reason and now has clear understanding?"

"Oh," he said. "Are you a stranger here?"

"Yes."

"Well, what makes you so intense about this thing?"

"I have someone in mind. Tell me, what is the first indication?"

"Why, it is marvelous that you should ask. See that man over there? That man became perfect in a moment, and we had had six men in charge of him. In a moment, he came to his senses. We had agreed together to pray at a certain time, and that man became as free as possible."

"What is the first indication?" I asked again.

"The first indication is that when a man is becoming sound in his mind, he wants to work."

And the first indication that you are becoming unsound is when you will not work! There is nothing wrong in work, but there is something wrong when we do not know how to live in it and over it.

When I finished talking with the coal carrier, he said, "I see!" What did he see? He saw that he could go on to his work, take hold of those bags of coal, put them on his back, and keep his mind on the Lord. When he did so, he became stronger every hour, and he carried a hundred bags out and finished promptly.

This is what God wants us to learn: *"Whatever you do, do all to the glory of God"* (1 Cor. 10:31). If you listen to the Word of God, it will make you strong. You will find out that whatever work you have to do will be made easier if you keep your mind *"stayed"* on the Lord (Isa. 26:3). Blessed is the one who has his mind focused on the Lord! We must see to it that in the world we are not moved.

KEPT IN PERFECT PEACE

One day, God revealed to me that if I had any trouble in my heart, I had missed His will. He showed me that if I had trouble in my heart, I had taken on something that did not belong to me, and I was out of the will of God. So I investigated it and found that it was true, according to His Word: *"You will keep him in perfect peace, whose mind is stayed on You, because he trusts in You"* (Isa. 26:3).

Interpretation of Tongues

God, in His great love toward us, has so distributed the power of His righteousness through our human bodies that the very activity now within us is a lift of praise. We adore Him, we thank Him, we praise Him, because he has "delivered us from the power of evil" and surrounded us by the power of light.

ATTRIBUTES OF SONSHIP

"That we should be called children of God!" (1 John 3:1). How are you to live? You are to live like a child of God. A child of God must have power over the power of the Devil (Luke 10:19). A child of God must behave in a fitting way. (See Ephesians 5:1–4.) A child of God must be *"temperate in all things"* (1 Cor. 9:25). A child of God must have the expression of the Master. He should be filled with tenderness and compassion. He should be filled with *"tender mercies"* (Col. 3:12). A child of God must excel in every way. God says to you more than you dare to say about yourself: "Behold, you are children of God." (See 1 John 3:3.) So do not be afraid. Take your stand, come into line, and say, "I will be a child of God."

God spoke, and the heavens yielded to His voice. He cried, *"This is My beloved Son, in whom I am well pleased. Hear Him!"* (Matt. 17:5). Afterward, Jesus always said, "I am the Son of God." Now, God comes to you and says, "Behold, you are the children of God!" Oh, that we could have a regiment of believers who would rise, claim their rights, stand erect with a holy vision, and be full of inward power, saying, "I am, by the grace of God, a child of God"!

"*Wisdom is justified by her children*" (Matt. 11:19). The man or woman who calls out to God does not need to fear. I stretch out my hand to you; you may, in many ways, have felt that you were never worthy; but God makes you worthy, and who can say that you are not worthy?

Interpretation of Tongues

It is the will of God to choose you. It is not your choice; it is the Lord's choice. Hear what He says: "I have chosen you, I have ordained you, that you should go forth bearing much fruit, and that your fruit should remain; for herein is your Father glorified, when you bring forth much fruit; so you will be my disciples."

SONS OF GOD NOW

*Beloved, **now** we are children of God; and it has not yet been revealed what we shall be, but we know that when He is revealed, we shall be like Him, for we shall see Him as He is.*
(1 John 3:2, emphasis added)

I am not talking about what we will be like after the second coming of Christ. I am dealing with the life that is in the believer now. I am dealing with our sonship in the earth. I am dealing with sonship; Son-likeness; what we are to be like in this world and what will take place when we live as children of God; how we can overcome the world; and what there is in our life in Christ that causes us to overcome the world.

"*Everyone who has this hope in Him*"—this hope of sonship; this hope of ministry; this hope of life-giving, of transmitting life—"*purifies himself, just as*

He is pure" (1 John 3:3). One thing that believers need to get to know is not how to quote Scripture but how the Scripture may be made effective by the Spirit, so that the Spirit may impart life as the Word is given. Jesus said, "My word brings life." (See John 5:24.) We need the Spirit to bring life into the believer, to impart life to him.

There is a deep secret concerning the imparting of life that involves the believer: *"Everyone who has this hope in Him **purifies himself,** just as He is pure"* (1 John 3:3, emphasis added). There is a lovely passage along this line in 1 Corinthians 11:31–32: *"If we would judge ourselves, we would not be judged. But when we are judged, we are chastened by the Lord, that we may not be condemned with the world."*

PEACE: NOT HYSTERIA OR NERVOUSNESS

This morning, a young woman asked a very important question about dealing with evil thoughts. I hope someday to specifically teach on how to discern evil spirits and how to deal with voices, because many people today are troubled by voices, and some people run here and there through the influence of voices. Certain people are so unsettled by voices that, instead of being the children of God, they seem to be gripped with a condition of hysteria or nervous breakdown.

Beloved, God wants to make you sound. God wants to make you restful. God wants to give you peace; He wants to cause you to live in the world with peace (John 14:27). The very first message the angels gave when they announced the birth of Christ was, *"On earth peace, goodwill toward men!"* (Luke 2:14). Jesus came to bring peace on earth and goodwill to men.

If you are not at peace, something is wrong. If you are not at rest, something has taken place that has robbed you of your rest. You must know that God desires you to be as much at peace as if you were in heaven.

The following statement is true; God hears me say it: I am as much at peace as if I were in the glory. I also declare to you that, according to the fact of *"the faith of the Son of God"* (Gal. 2:20 KJV) in me, I am not troubled by any pain or sickness in my body. I am free from everything that means weakness.

There is a redemption in Christ, a fullness of redemption, that will make us free from the power of sin and from the powers of evil and evil thoughts, so that we will reign in the world over demonic powers, not being subject to them, but making everything subject to us. (See Luke 10:17.)

I want you to come into a royal place, to be purified *"just as He is pure"* (1 John 3:3). Most people fail to come into perfect line with God because they allow their own reasoning or their own troubled thoughts to nullify the power that God has.

Why do we always bring up the past? Why, no one can forgive himself. The best people in the world would give anything if they could forgive themselves for what they have done. You would give the world if you could forgive yourself, but you cannot; you feel ashamed.

One thing is sure: you cannot forget the evil things that you have done. Another thing is also sure: the Devil will not let you forget. But there is a third thing that is true: God has forgotten our sins (Isa. 43:25; Jer. 31:34), and we have to decide whether we will believe ourselves, the Devil, or God. Which are you going to believe? "When He forgives, He forgets."

On the authority of your believing God's Word, I can bring you into a new place. There are wonderful things to achieve along the line of faith that dares to believe God. *"Only believe"* (Mark 5:36)! *"According to your faith let it be to you"* (Matt. 9:29).

Master over Evil Thoughts

The question the young woman asked this morning was this: "What is the condition of a person who is always troubled with evil thoughts? How is he going to stand? What position is he in when these evil thoughts are always following him?"

Evil thoughts are from Satan. Satan does not know your thoughts. Satan does not know your desires. God hides these things from him. God can *"search the heart"* and *"test the mind"* (Jer. 17:10), but a stranger never interferes with them. Nobody knows you but God. The Devil never has a chance of knowing you.

So what does the Devil do? First, let us see that he came to Jesus, and when he came, all the evil things he suggested could not arouse a single thing in our Lord. (See, for example, Matthew 4:1–11.) The Devil came and found nothing in Him (John 14:30). So when does the Devil find anything in you? When he suggests a thought in order to bring some thought out of you, and he gets you the moment he does. But if you are delivered by the blood and made holy, the Devil cannot arouse you. Nevertheless, if you are troubled when he suggests an evil thought, you are in a good place; but if you are not troubled, you are in a bad place.

Suppose he is continually attacking you in this manner. Is there a way to overcome it? Of course there is. How can you deal with it? Say to him, "Did Jesus come in the flesh?" And the Evil One will say, "No." No demon power out of hell or in hell has ever been willing to say that Jesus came in the flesh. So when he says "No," you can say, "Get behind me, Satan! I rebuke you in the name of Jesus." (See 1 John 4:2–4.) Oh, it is wonderful for the child of God to be brought into liberty, power, blessing, and strength, until he lives on the earth purified like the Lord.

Do you believe you can ever be like Him? Cheer up, now. Don't measure yourself by yourself, or you will be defeated. Measure yourself by the life of the Lord at work within you, and put your hope in Him. *"Everyone who has this hope in Him purifies himself, just as He is pure"* (1 John 3:3). Then you will be in a wonderful place of dominion over sin and evil.

A DANCE TURNED INTO A PRAYER MEETING

There are wonderful things about this life in Christ. I would like to bring you to a place where it is so easy to triumph over the powers of the Devil, even when you are right in the midst of them.

I was traveling on a ship between England and Australia, and about the third day out, they were asking me, along with everybody else, to join with them in an entertainment. We were then running a mission according to holiness principles, and we would not allow a teacher in our Sunday school who went to questionable amusements, so we never participated in what they call entertainment. But these people came to me and said, "We want to know if you will join us in an entertainment."

So I had to go quietly to the Lord. "Can I?" I asked Him. I had the sweetest rest about it; it was all right. So I said, "Yes, I will be in the entertainment." They said, "What can you do?" "I can sing," I answered. Then they said to me, "Well, we have a very large program, and we would like to put you down, and we would like to give you the song." "Oh!" I said. "My song will be given just before I sing. So you cannot put it down until I am to sing."

They did not care for that very much, but they allowed it. Then they came to me again and said, "We are very anxious to know what place in the program you would like to appear." "What are you going to have?" I asked. "How are you going to finish up?" "Oh," they said, "we have all kinds of things." There wasn't a thing the Devil could arrange that wasn't there. "Well, how are you going to finish up?" I asked again. "We are going to finish up with a dance," they replied. "Put me down just before the dance," I said.

Some ministers were attending the entertainment, and when I went there, I felt so sorry to find these clergymen trying to satisfy a giddy, godless lot of people, and trying to fit in. My turn came. A young woman who was scantily dressed came up to play the piano for me. I gave her the music. "Oh!" she said. "I never—I never could play that kind of music." "Now, don't you be troubled," I said. "I have both music and words." And I sang,

> If I could only tell it as I know it,
> My Redeemer who has done so much for me;
> If I could only tell you how He loves you,
> I am sure that you would make Him yours
>   today.

> Could I tell it? Could I tell it?

I never could tell it. All around the room, people were weeping. The dance was put off; they couldn't have a dance. But we had lots of prayer meetings, and some fine young men gave themselves to Jesus.

Beloved, we must be in the world, not of it (John 17:11, 14). What a lovely thing Jesus said to the Father: *"I do not pray that You should take them out of the world, but that You should keep them from the evil one"* (v. 15). Can He do it? He can do it; He has a way to do it. You say, How does He do it?

> Let the waves wash me,
> Let the waves cleanse me,
> Lord, in Your power
> Let them roll over me.

How the blood of Jesus can cleanse! How He can make us clean! How He can stimulate faith and change our powerless condition!

SIN DETHRONED

Now I want to put before you some very difficult things. There are some things that are so difficult and yet so easy. Their difficulty rises and brings perplexity because we do not see that the Lord is greater than everything. We have to see that the Master's hand is so much greater than our hand, and that His ways over us are so much greater than our ways.

"Whoever commits sin also commits lawlessness, and sin is lawlessness. And you know that He was manifested to take away our sins, and in Him there is no sin" (1 John 3:4–5). There is to be no sin in us. We are to purify ourselves as He is pure (1 John 3:3). Sin has been destroyed. Do not be afraid to claim your

position in Christ. *"Sin shall not have dominion over you"* (Rom. 6:14). Do not be afraid to see the Word of God. It is true. You are *"dead indeed to sin, but alive to God"* (v. 11). Being dead to sin and being alive to God are the same thing.

As sin had *"reigned unto death"* (Rom. 5:21 KJV), so now Christ comes and reigns over you in life, and you reign in life over sin, disease, and the Devil; you reign over *"principalities and powers"* (Col. 2:15); you reign in Christ.

Where is Christ manifested? He is manifested in our flesh, to destroy the sinful passions of our bodies, to bring carnality to an end (Gal. 5:24), to bring everything of human depravity to a place of defeat. When Christ is in the body, sin is dethroned. Sin shall not reign over you (Rom. 6:14).

Believe that God is bringing you to the place where Christ is manifested in you. This place is a dethronement of human helplessness; it is an enthronement of Christ's righteousness in us. Christ comes in and begins to rule over our human bodies according to His plan. What is His plan? *"Everyone who has this hope in Him purifies himself, just as He is pure"* (1 John 3:3).

Why is this so? There are several steps on the ladder: *"Whoever abides in Him does not sin"* (v. 6). Get that established in your heart as one of the steps. Now let's go a little farther by taking the next step: *"Whoever sins has neither seen Him nor known Him. Little children, let no one deceive you. He who practices righteousness is righteous, just as He is righteous"* (1 John 3:6–7). The third step is found in verse 8: *"He who sins is of the devil, for the devil has sinned from the beginning. For this purpose the Son of God was manifested, that He might destroy the works of the devil."*

113

Where was Christ manifested? In your flesh, *"that He might destroy the works of the devil."* Where? Outside of you? No, in your flesh, where there was *"nothing good"* (Rom. 7:18). He destroyed everything that was not good, came and ruled there, and is there now.

Now I give you one of the hardest problems of the Scriptures, and yet the most beautiful position of the Scriptures. It is a keynote of possibility. It is like being on Mount Pisgah and looking over into the Promised Land, with all the fruits of Canaan at your feet. (See Deuteronomy 34:1–4 KJV.) God will make the grapes of Eshcol very beautiful as you enter into this sublime position of faith. (See Numbers 13:23.)

Our Conquering Position

"And everyone who has this hope in Him purifies himself, just as He is pure" (1 John 3:3). *"Whoever has been born of God does not sin, for His seed remains in him; and he cannot sin, because he has been born of God"* (v. 9). I want to explain these verses to you in order to help you. Through these truths, many people, on the authority of God's Word, will be made strong over the power of sin. Sin will not meet you any longer as a master (Rom. 6:14); you will meet it as a conqueror, dethroning it. Here is your conquering position: *"Everyone who has this hope in Him purifies himself, just as He is pure."*

This is the seed; this is the seed of life, the seed of the Son of God. This is the nature of the Son of God. The nature of the Son of God is purity, and for him who *"purifies himself,"* who has obtained this possession of the life of the Son of God—the eternal seed, the purifying position, the incorruptible power—this seed remains in him, and he cannot sin. The purifying seed makes you hate sin. One of the purposes of the salvation of the world is that people would hate sin.

Look at the Master. Have you ever really seen Jesus? God highly exalted Him and gave Him a name above every name (Phil. 2:9). Why? Jesus hated iniquity. What is the difference between hating sin, and knowing that sin is there but passing it by without seeing it or speaking to it? The latter position will never save you. You have to have a righteous indignation against the powers of evil and the Devil; you need to be continually purified, and then you will get to the place where you cannot sin.

This is a glorious position of arrival. This is a blessed place of exit. This is a glorious place of overcoming. This is a place of rest for your feet. This is a great place for endowment of power, for holiness is power, and sin is weakness and defeat.

GOD CLAIMS YOU AS HIS OWN

You are so intense. Your hearts are longing, and your souls are thirsty. You are waking up to the fact that God has chosen you to be His children, to be pure, to have power, to have righteousness. *"Sin shall not have dominion"* (Rom. 6:14); disease will be dethroned; God will claim you as His own. You will be the sons of God with power. (See Romans 1:4.) Who says so? Your Father in heaven. You will be the sons of God, with your sins dethroned and your hearts aflame! Look where God is bringing you. I will read these words to you to strengthen your hearts to enter a new place. This is the place, a wonderful place of covenant and blessing:

And by this we know that we are of the truth, and shall assure our hearts before Him. For if our heart condemns us, God is greater than our heart, and knows all things. Beloved, if our heart does not condemn us, we have confidence toward God. And whatever we ask we receive from Him, because we keep His commandments and do those things that are pleasing in His sight. (1 John 3:19–22)

"Do Not Be Afraid; Only Believe"

I believe that it is in the purpose and will of God that we look at a passage from the fifth chapter of Mark's gospel. My message is based on the words, *"Do not be afraid; only believe"* (Mark 5:36).

HEAR IN FAITH

This is one of those marvelous, glorious truths of Scripture that is written to help us. It enables us to believe, as we see the almightiness of God and also our own possibilities—not only of entering in by faith, but also of becoming partakers of the blessing God wants to give us. My message is about faith. Because some do not hear in faith, they do not profit at all from what they hear. There is a hearing of faith and a hearing that means nothing more than listening to words.

I implore you to see to it that everything that is done may bring not only blessing to you, but also strength and character. I want you to see the wonderfulness and goodness of God. I want to impress upon you the importance of believing what the Scripture says, and I may have many things to relate about people who dared to believe God until His Word came to pass.

This passage from Mark 5 is a wonderful Scripture passage. In fact, all of the Word of God is wonderful. It is an everlasting Word, a Word of power, a Word of health, a Word of substance, a Word of life. It gives life to the very nature of the one who lays hold of it, if he believes. I want you to understand that there is a need for the Word of God. But many times it is a need that brings us the blessing.

ON THE VERGE OF DEATH

Why am I here tonight? Because God delivered me when no other hand could do it. I stand before you as one who was given up by everybody, one whom no one could help.

Let me give you a little background to my story. I was earnest and zealous for the salvation of souls. If you had been in Bradford, England, the town where I lived, you would know. Our ministry had police protection for nearly twenty years in the best thoroughfare in the city, and in my humble way, with my dear wife, who was all on fire for God, I was ministering in the open air. Was I full of zeal? Yes. But one night, about thirty years ago, I was carried home helpless. My wife and I knew very little about divine healing, but we prayed through. It has been more than thirty years since God healed me. I am sixty-five years old, and I am fresher, in better health, and more fit for work than I was in my thirties. It is a most wonderful experience when the life of God becomes the life of man. The divine power that sweeps through the organism, cleansing the blood, makes the man fresh every day. The life of God is resurrection power.

Let me tell you exactly how my healing occurred. When I was brought home helpless, we prayed all night. We did all we knew to do. At ten o'clock the next morning, I said to my wife, "This must be my last roll call." We had five children around us. I tell you, it was not an easy thing to face our circumstances. I told my wife to do as she thought best, but the poor thing didn't know what to do. She called a physician, who examined me, shook his head, and said, "It is impossible for anything to be done for your husband; I am absolutely helpless. He has appendicitis, and you have waited too long. His system will not stand an operation. A few hours, at best, will finish him."

What the doctor said to my wife was true. He left her and said that he would come back again, but that he couldn't give her any hope. When he was nicely out of the house, an old lady and a young man came in who knew how to pray. The young man put his knees on the bed and said, "Come out, you devil, in the name of Jesus." It was a good job. I had no time to argue, and instantly I was free. Oh, hallelujah! I was as free as I am now.

I have never believed that any person ought to be in bed in the daytime, so I jumped up and went downstairs. My wife said, "Oh, are you up?" "I am all right, wife; it is all right now," I said. I had some men working for me, and she said none of them had shown up that morning. So I picked up my tools and went to work. Then the doctor came. He walked up the stairs, and my wife called, "Doctor, doctor, he is out!"

"What?" he said. "Yes," she answered, "he went to work." "Oh," he said, "you will never see him alive again. They will bring him home a corpse." But as you can see, I am not a corpse!

Oh, when God does anything, it is done forever! And God wants you to know that He wants to do something in you forever. There are people in this place who have been delivered from appendicitis in these meetings. I have laid my hands on people with appendicitis when doctors were in the place, and God has healed them.

GOD CAN USE YOU

I will tell you one more incident before I move on. It will stir up your faith. I am not here to be on exhibition; I am here to impart divine truth to you concerning the Word of God, so that, after I leave, you can do the same things that I have done. I went to Switzerland, and after I had been there for some weeks, a brother said, "Aren't you going to the meeting tonight?" "No," I said, "I have been at it all this time; you can take charge tonight." "What shall we do?" he asked. "Do?" I said; "Paul the apostle left people to do the work and went on to another place. I have been here long enough now. You do the work." So he went to the meeting. When he came back, he said, "We had a wonderful time." "What happened?" I asked. He said, "I invited them all up, took off my coat, rolled up my sleeves, and prayed. They were all healed. I did just as you did."

Jesus said, *"I give you the authority...over all the power of the enemy"* (Luke 10:19). Jesus' disciples entered into people's houses and healed the sick who were there. The ministry of divine operation in us is wonderful, but who would take it upon himself to say, "I can do this or that"? If it is God, it is all right, but if it is you, it is all wrong. When you are weak, then you are strong. (See 2 Corinthians 12:9–10.) When you are strong in your own strength, you are weak. You must realize this and live only in the place where the power of God rests upon you, and where the Spirit moves within you. Then God will mightily manifest His power, and you will say, as Jesus said, *"The Spirit of the Lord is upon me"* (Luke 4:18 KJV).

DESPERATE PARENTS

God brings a remarkable, glorious fact to my mind tonight: the healing of a helpless little girl, recorded in the fifth chapter of Mark. The physicians had failed. I imagine the girl's mother said to the father, "There is only one hope—if you can see Jesus! If you can meet Jesus, our daughter will live." Do you think it is possible for anybody in this city of Washington, D.C., to go looking for Jesus without seeing Him? Is it possible to think about Jesus without Jesus drawing near? No.

This father knew the power there is in the name of Jesus: *"In My name they will cast out demons"* (Mark 16:17). But we must be sure that we truly know that name, for in Acts 19, the seven sons of Sceva said to the man who was possessed with a devil, *"We exorcise you by the Jesus whom Paul preaches"* (v. 13). The evil spirit said, *"Jesus I know, and Paul I know; but who are you?"* (v. 15). Yes, the Devil knows every believer—and the seven sons of Sceva nearly lost their lives. The evil power came upon them, and they barely escaped.

There is more to casting out demons than repeating the name of Jesus; there is the nature of that name within you. Even more than that, there is the Divine Personality within the human life who has come to take up His abode. When Christ becomes all in all in you, then God works through you. The key is the life and the power of God. God works through the life.

The Lord is that life. By the Holy Spirit, the ministry of that life and the power in the ministry bring every believer into such a place of divine relationship that He mightily lives in us and enables us to overcome the powers of the Enemy. The Lord healed that child as the parents got a vision of Jesus. The word of the Lord "[did] *not come with observation*" (Luke 17:20), but with divine, mighty power. As an oracle by the power of the Spirit, it worked in men and women until they were created anew by this new life divine. We have to see that when this divine word comes to us by the power of the Holy Spirit, we speak according to the will of God—not with man's wisdom, but with divine minds operated by the word of God; not as channels only, but as oracles of the Spirit.

THE SYNAGOGUE RULER AND THE BELIEVING WOMAN

Let us now read the passage of Scripture from which this remarkable account of the healing of the helpless little girl comes:

> *And behold, one of the rulers of the synagogue came, Jairus by name. And when he saw Him, he fell at His feet and begged Him earnestly, saying, "My little daughter lies at the point of death. Come and lay Your hands on her, that she may be healed, and she will live." So Jesus*

went with him, and a great multitude followed
Him and thronged Him. Now a certain woman
had a flow of blood for twelve years, and had
suffered many things from many physicians.
She had spent all that she had and was no
better, but rather grew worse. When she heard
about Jesus, she came behind Him in the crowd
and touched His garment. For she said, "If only
I may touch His clothes, I shall be made well."
Immediately the fountain of her blood was dried
up, and she felt in her body that she was healed
of the affliction. And Jesus, immediately knowing in Himself that power had gone out of Him,
turned around in the crowd and said, "Who
touched My clothes?" But His disciples said to
Him, "You see the multitude thronging You, and
You say, 'Who touched Me?'" And He looked
around to see her who had done this thing.
But the woman, fearing and trembling, knowing what had happened to her, came and fell
down before Him and told Him the whole truth.
And He said to her, "Daughter, your faith has
made you well. Go in peace, and be healed of
your affliction." While He was still speaking,
some came from the ruler of the synagogue's
house who said, "Your daughter is dead. Why
trouble the Teacher any further?" As soon as
Jesus heard the word that was spoken, He said
to the ruler of the synagogue, "Do not be afraid;
only believe." And He permitted no one to follow
Him except Peter, James, and John the brother
of James. Then He came to the house of the
ruler of the synagogue, and saw a tumult and
those who wept and wailed loudly. When He
came in, He said to them, "Why make this commotion and weep? The child is not dead, but

*sleeping." And they ridiculed Him. But when
He had put them all outside, He took the father
and the mother of the child, and those who
were with Him, and entered where the child was
lying. Then He took the child by the hand, and
said to her, "Talitha, cumi," which is translated, "Little girl, I say to you, arise." Immediately the girl arose and walked, for she was
twelve years of age. And they were overcome
with great amazement. But He commanded
them strictly that no one should know it, and
said that something should be given her to eat.*
(Mark 5:22–43)

As the ruler of the synagogue sought Jesus, he
worshiped Him (v. 22). How the people gathered
around Him! How everybody listened to what He had
to say! He spoke with authority and power, *"not as the
scribes"* (Matt. 7:29), and He was clothed with divine
glory.

Let me tell you another incident to emphasize
what I want you to understand about the ruler
of the synagogue and his daughter. A young man
was preaching in a marketplace. At the close of the
address, an atheist came and said, "There have been
five Jesuses. Tell us which one it is that you preach."
He answered, *"Him who was raised from the dead"*
(Rom. 7:4). There is only One who rose from the dead.
There is only one Jesus who lives. And as He lives, we
live also. Glory to God! We are risen with Him, we are
living with Him, and we will reign with Him.

As this synagogue ruler drew near the crowd, he
went up to Jesus and said, *"My little daughter lies
at the point of death. Come and lay Your hands on
her, that she may be healed, and she will live"* (Mark

5:23). "I will come," Jesus said. (See verse 24.) What a beautiful assurance. But as they were going along the road, they were met by a woman who had had a flow of blood for twelve years. When this trouble had started, she had sought help from many physicians. She had had some money, but the physicians had taken it all and left her worse off than when they had found her (v. 26).

Do you have any doctors around here who do the same thing? When I was a plumber, I had to finish my work before I got the money, and I didn't always get it then. I think that if there were an arrangement whereby no doctor would get his fee until he cured the patient, not as many people would die.

This woman had had twelve years of sickness. She needed someone now who could heal without money, for she was bankrupt and helpless.

Jesus comes to people who are withered up, diseased, lame, or crippled in all kinds of ways. When He comes, there is liberty for the captive, opening of eyes for the blind, and opening of ears for the deaf. I imagine that many people had said to this woman, "If you had only been with us today! We saw the most marvelous things—the crooked made straight, the lame made to walk, the blind made to see." And the woman who had been sick for twelve years said, "Oh, you make me feel that if I could only see Him, I would be healed." Their words strengthened her faith, and it became firm. She had a purpose within her.

Faith is a mighty power. Faith will reach at everything. When real faith comes into operation, you will not say, "I don't feel much better." Faith says, "I am whole." Faith doesn't say, "I have a lame leg." Faith says, "My leg is all right."

SEEING THROUGH THE EYES OF FAITH

A young woman with a goiter came to one of my meetings to be prayed for. In a testimony meeting, she said, "I do praise the Lord for healing my goiter." She went home and said to her mother, "Oh, Mother, when the man prayed for me, God healed my goiter." For twelve months, she went around telling everybody how God had healed her goiter. Then I came to minister there again, and people said, "How big that lady's goiter is!" There came a time for testimonies. She jumped up and said, "I was here twelve months ago, and God healed me of my goiter. It has been such a marvelous twelve months!" When she went home, her family said, "You should have seen the people today when you testified that God had healed your goiter. They think there is something wrong with you. If you will go upstairs and look in the mirror, you will see that the goiter is bigger than it ever was." She went upstairs, but she didn't look in the mirror. She got down on her knees and said, "Oh, Lord, let all the people know, just as You have let me know, how wonderfully You have healed me." The next morning, her neck was as perfect as any neck you ever saw. Faith never looks. Faith praises God, saying, "It is done!"

JESUS HEALS THE BELIEVING WOMAN AND THE RULER'S DAUGHTER

Let us continue now with the biblical account of these healings. The poor helpless woman who had been growing weaker and weaker for twelve years pushed into the crowded thoroughfare when she knew that Jesus was in the midst. She was stirred to the depths, and she pushed through and touched Him. If you will believe God and touch Him, you will go out of this place as well as can be. Jesus is the Healer!

Now, listen! Some people substitute touching the Lord for faith. The Lord did not want that woman to believe that the touch had done it. As soon as she touched Him, she felt that power had gone through her, which was true. When the Israelites were bitten by fiery serpents in the wilderness, God's Word said through Moses, "He who looks at the bronze serpent on the pole will be healed." (See Numbers 21:8.) The look made it possible for God to do it. But the people who looked had to have faith that God's Word was true. Now, did the touch heal the woman? No, the touch meant something more—it was evidence of a living faith. Jesus said, *"Your **faith** has made you well"* (Mark 5:34, emphasis added). If God would just move on us to believe, no one would leave this place tonight sick.

As soon as this woman, who was in the street with the whole crowd around her, began to testify, the Devil came. The Devil is always in a testimony meeting. Even when the *"sons of God"* gathered together before the Lord in the time of Job, Satan was there (Job 1:6). So how did the Enemy come into this situation with the believing woman and the synagogue ruler? While the woman was speaking with Jesus, some people came rushing from the house of Jairus and said, "It is no use now; your daughter is dead. This Jesus can do nothing for a dead daughter. Your wife needs you at home." (See Mark 5:35.) But Jesus said, *"Do not be afraid; only believe"* (v. 36).

He spoke the word just in time! Jesus is never late. When the tumult is the worst, the pain most severe, the cancer gripping the body, then come the words, *"Only believe."* When everything seems as though it will fail, when everything is practically hopeless, the Word of God comes to us: *"Only believe."*

When Jesus came to the ruler's house, He found a lot of people weeping and wailing. People mourn for the dead, but as for me, I have taken my last wreath to the cemetery. *"To be absent from the body* [is] *to be present with the Lord"* (2 Cor. 5:8), and if you believe that, you will never need to take another wreath to the cemetery. It is unbelief that mourns. If you have faith that your departed loved ones are with the Lord, you will never need to take another flower to the grave. They are not there. Hallelujah!

These people were standing around weeping, wailing, and howling. Jesus said, *"Why make this commotion and weep? The child is not dead, but sleeping"* (Mark 5:39).

There is a wonderful word that God wants you to hear. Jesus said, *"I am the resurrection and the life"* (John 11:25). The believer may fall asleep in Christ, but the believer doesn't die. Oh, that people would understand the deep things of God; the whole situation would be changed! Then they would look with a glorious hope to the day when the Lord will return. What does the Bible say? *"God will bring with Him those who sleep in Jesus"* (1 Thess. 4:14). Jesus knew that. *"He said to them, '...The child is not dead, but sleeping.' And they ridiculed Him* ["laughed Him to scorn," KJV]*"* (Mark 5:39–40). These wailers showed their insincerity in that they could turn from wailing to mocking.

But Jesus took the father and mother of the girl, and, going into the room where she was, took her hand and said, *"Little girl, I say to you, arise"* (v. 41). And the child sat up. Praise the Lord! And Jesus said, "Give her something to eat." (See verse 43.)

"Do Not Be Afraid; Only Believe"

YOU CAN KNOW THAT YOU ARE SAVED

Oh, the remarkableness of our Lord Jesus! I want to impress upon you tonight the importance of realizing that He is in the midst of us. No person needs to go away without knowing not only that he is saved, but also that God can live in these bodies of ours. You are begotten, the moment you believe, unto *"a living hope"* (1 Pet. 1:3).

I wonder if anyone in this place is a stranger to this new birth into life. Jesus said, *"He who believes in Me **has** everlasting life"* (John 6:47, emphasis added). You have eternal life the moment you believe. The first life is temporal, natural, material, but in the new birth, you exist as long as God exists—forever! We are begotten by an incorruptible power, by the Word of God (1 Pet. 1:23). The new birth is unto righteousness. You are begotten by God the moment that you believe.

We are talking about divine things tonight. Oh, the wonderful adaptability of God, for Him to come right into this place! Those of you who have not been satisfied, who have sought salvation and have had good impressions, perhaps, but have never known the reality and joy of the new birth, let me enlist you. The Word of God says, *"Before they call, I will answer"* (Isa. 65:24). The raising of your hand is a sign of your heart's desire. God always saves through the heart. He who believes in his heart and confesses with his mouth will be saved (Rom. 10:9).

Jesus is here tonight to loose those who are bound. If you are suffering in your body, He will heal you now as we pray. He is saying to every sin-sick soul, to every disease-stricken one, *"Do not be afraid; only believe"* (Mark 5:36).

We Mean Business with God

There is a power in God's Word that brings life where death is. *"Only believe"* (Mark 5:36). *"Only believe."* Jesus said that the time will come when *"the dead will hear the voice of the Son of God; and those who hear will live"* (John 5:25). For he who believes this Word, *"all things are possible to him who believes"* (Mark 9:23). The life of the Son is in the Word, and all who are saved can preach this Word. This Word frees us from death and corruption; it is life in the nature. Jesus *"brought life and immortality to light through the gospel"* (2 Tim. 1:10).

We can never exhaust the Word; it is so abundant. *"There is a river whose streams...make glad the city of God"* (Ps. 46:4); its source is in the glory. The essence of its life is God. The life of Jesus embodied is its manifested power.

Interpretation of Tongues

Jesus Himself has come into death and has given us the victory; the victorious Son of

131

God in humanity overcomes, He who succors the needy. Immortality produced in mortality has changed the situation for us. This is life indeed and the end of death, Christ having "brought life and immortality to life through the Gospel."

THE NEW CHURCH ESTABLISHED

We have a wonderful subject tonight because of its manifestation of the nature of the church, for in God's first church, no lie could live. The new church that the Holy Spirit is building has no lie, but purity and *"holiness to the LORD"* (Jer. 2:3). I see the new church established in the breath of the Lord. God is working in a supernatural way, making faces shine with His glory, creating people so in likeness with Him that they love what is right, hate iniquity and evil, and deeply reverence Him, so that a lie is unable to remain in their midst.

"There is therefore now no condemnation to those who are in Christ Jesus, who do not walk according to the flesh, but according to the Spirit" (Rom. 8:1). No one can condemn you. Many may try, but God's Word says,

> *Who shall bring a charge against God's elect? It is God who justifies. Who is he who condemns? It is Christ who died, and furthermore is also risen, who is even at the right hand of God, who also makes intercession for us.* (Rom. 8:33–34)

Will Jesus condemn the sheep for whom He died? He died to save men, and He saves all who believe.

God is purifying our hearts by faith. God has come forth, clothing us with His Spirit's might, living in the blaze of this glorious day—for there is nothing greater than the Gospel.

In Acts 5, we read that Ananias and Sapphira were moved to bring an offering (v. 1). The day will come when we will consider nothing as our own, because we will be so taken up with the Lord. The church will ripen into coming glory. The first day was a measure; the latter day was to be more generous.

Ananias and Sapphira sold a possession; it was their own, but when it was sold, it looked like so much money. They reasoned, "The Pentecostal order is new; it might dry up." So they agreed to give a part and reserve the other (v. 2). Satan is very subtle. Many people miss the greatest things by drawing aside. Let us pay our vows to the Lord (Ps. 116:14, 18).

"But Peter said, 'Ananias, why has Satan filled your heart to lie to the Holy Spirit and keep back part of the price of the land for yourself?'" (Acts 5:3). The moment Ananias and Sapphira lied to the Holy Spirit by presenting only a portion of the money to the apostles, they were struck down (vv. 2–11).

God has shown us a new order of the Spirit in this Holy Spirit baptism. One day, when I came into my house, my wife said, "Did you come in at the front door?" I said, "No, I came in at the back." "Oh," she said. "At the front you would have seen a crowd and a man with little clothing on, crying out, 'I have committed the unpardonable sin!'"

As I went to the door, God whispered to me, "This is what I baptized you in the Spirit for." The man came in crying, "I have committed the unpardonable sin!" I said, "You lying devil, come out, in Jesus' name." The man said, "What is it? I am free. Thank God, I never committed the unpardonable sin." The moment the lying spirit was gone, he was able to speak the truth.

I realized then the power in the baptism of the Holy Spirit. It was the Spirit who said, "This is what I baptized you for," and I believe we ought to be in the place where we will always be able to understand the mind of the Spirit amid all the other voices in the world.

PURITY OF LIFE BEFORE GOD

When Ananias and Sapphira died, great fear came upon the church (Acts 5:5, 11). It demonstrated the believers' love for God in that they feared to grieve Him. Why, they could ask and receive anything from God.

The church is to be of one accord, with perfect faithfulness, love, oneness, and consolation. God can lift the church into a place of manifested reconciliation and oneness, until the Devil has no power in our midst, and God is smiling on us all the time.

"And through the hands of the apostles many signs and wonders were done among the people" (v. 12). A purity of life before God means a manifested power among men, with multitudes gathered into the kingdom of God. God has mightily blessed the work at Elim Tabernacle, where this meeting is taking place. Those of you who are still lingering outside the kingdom, yield to God. Get *"clean hands"* and a right purpose (Ps. 24:4), join what is holy and on fire, and mean business for God.

"And believers were increasingly added to the Lord, multitudes of both men and women" (Acts 5:14). Oh, for this kind of revival, God breaking forth everywhere and London swept by the power of God! There must be a great moving among us, a oneness of heart and soul, and revival is sure to come as God moves upon the people.

> *They brought the sick out into the streets and laid them on beds and couches, that at least the shadow of Peter passing by might fall on some of them. Also a multitude gathered from the surrounding cities to Jerusalem, bringing sick people and those who were tormented by unclean spirits, and they were all healed.*
>
> (Acts 5:15–16)

Unity has the effect of manifesting the work of God every time. Glory to God, it is so lovely. The people had such a living faith; they were of one heart, one mind. They thought, "Oh, if only Peter's shadow passes over our sick ones, God will heal them."

Have faith. God will heal the land. Oneness of heart and mind on the part of the church means signs and wonders in all lands. *"Whatever things you ask when you pray, believe that you receive them, and you will have them"* (Mark 11:24). *"Only believe"* (Mark 5:36). I see, beloved, that we need to get more love, and the Lord will do it. How the Master can move among the needy and perishing when He has the right of way in the church!

The finest thing is persecution. We must have a ministry that makes the people glad and the Devil mad. Never mind if the people run away, for conviction is within, and God has them. And if the people are glad, the Lord also has them, so it works both ways. Don't be disturbed at anything. Remember that it was written of the Master, *"Zeal for Your house has eaten Me up"* (John 2:17). We need to have a melting, moving, broken condition—*"as poor, yet making many rich; as having nothing, and yet possessing all things"* (2 Cor. 6:10). Let us be in harmony with the divine plan, having knowledge cemented with love, death to the old nature having perfect place in us, so that the life-power can be manifested.

I once went for weekend meetings, and when I arrived on Saturday night, it was snowing hard, and the man meeting me stood at the door of the hall laden with packages. As we walked home, when we reached the first lamppost, I said, "Brother, are you baptized in the Holy Spirit?" Then I said, "Say you will be tonight." As we went along, at every lamppost (nearly a hundred), I repeated the question, "Say you will be baptized tonight." So he began wishing I was not staying at his house. At last we reached the gate to his house. I jumped over it and said, "Now, don't you come in here unless you say you will be baptized with the Holy Spirit tonight." "Oh," he said, "I feel so funny, but I will say it." We went in. I asked his wife, "Are you baptized in the Holy Spirit?" She said, "Oh, I want to be—but supper is ready, come in." I said, "No supper until you are both baptized in the Holy Spirit."

Did God answer? Oh yes, soon they were both speaking in tongues. Now, I believe that God will baptize you. Put up your hands and ask Him to. Also, those seeking healing and salvation, do the same, and God will meet you, every one. Amen.

After You Have Received Power

I n Acts 1:8, we read, *"You shall receive power when the Holy Spirit has come upon you."* Oh, the power of the Holy Spirit—the power that quickens, reveals, and prevails! I love the thought that Jesus wanted all His people to have power, that He wanted all men to be overcomers. Nothing but this power of the Holy Spirit will do it—power over sin, power over sickness, power over the Devil, power over all the powers of the Devil (Luke 10:19)!

In order to understand what it means to have power, two things are necessary: one is to have *"ears to hear"* (Matt. 11:15), and the other is to have hearts to receive. Every born-again saint of God who is filled with the Spirit has a real revelation of this truth: *"He who is in you is greater than he who is in the world"* (1 John 4:4). I say this with as much audacity as I please: I know evil spirits are in abundance and in multitudes; Jesus cast them out as legion. (See Mark 5:2–15; Luke 8:26–35.) The believer, because of the

Spirit who is in him, has the power to cast out the evil spirit. It *must* be so; God wants us to have this power in us; we must be able to destroy Satan's power wherever we go.

ALWAYS READY

After the Holy Spirit comes upon you, you have power. I believe a great mistake is made in these days by people waiting and waiting after they have received. After you have received, it is, *"Go"* (Mark 16:15). It is not, "Sit still," but *"Go into all the world and preach the gospel"* (v. 15). We will make serious havoc of the whole thing if we turn back again and crawl into a corner seeking something we already have. I want you to see that God depends on us in these last days. There is no room for anyone to boast, and the person who goes around saying, "Look at me, for I am somebody," is of no value whatever. God will not often work through such a person. He will have a people who glorify Him. He is doing what He can with what He has, but we are so unwilling to move in the plan of God that He has to grind us many times to get us where He can use us.

Jesus was so filled with the Holy Spirit that He stood in the place where He was always ready. He was always in the attitude where He brought victory out of every opportunity. The power of the Holy Spirit is within us, but it can be manifested only as we go in obedience to the opportunity before us. I believe if you wait until you think you have power after you have received the Holy Spirit, you will never know you have it. Don't you know that the child of God who has the baptism is inhabited by the Spirit? Remember the incident in the Bible where the Jews were going to

stone Jesus? He slipped away from them, and shortly
afterward, He healed the man with the blind eyes.
(See John 8:48–9:7.) Slipping away from the crowd
that was trying to kill Him, He showed forth His
power. Some people might think that Jesus should
have run away altogether, but He stopped to heal.
This thought has comforted me over and over again.

One day, as I was waiting for a streetcar, I stepped
into a shoemaker's shop. I had not been there long
when I saw a man with a green shade over his eyes.
He was crying pitifully and was in great agony; it
was heartbreaking. The shoemaker told me that the
inflammation was intensely burning and injuring his
eyes. I jumped up and went to the man and said, "You
devil, come out of this man in the name of Jesus."
Instantly, the man said, "It is all gone; I can see now."
That is the only scriptural way: to begin to work at
once, and to preach afterward. *"Jesus began both to do
and teach"* (Acts 1:1).

GRACE ABOUNDING

You will find, as the days go by, that the miracles
and healings will be manifested. Because the Master
was *"touched with the feeling of* [the] *infirmities"*
(Heb. 4:15 KJV) of the multitudes, they instantly gathered around Him to hear what He had to say concerning the Word of God. However, I would rather see
one man saved than ten thousand people healed. If
you should ask me why, I would call your attention
to the Word, which says, *"There was a certain rich
man who…fared sumptuously every day"* (Luke 16:19).
Now, we don't hear of this man having any diseases,
but the Word says that, after he died, *"being in tor-
ments in Hades* ["hell," KJV], *he lifted up his eyes"*

(Luke 16:23). We also read that there was a poor man who was full of sores, and that, after he died, he *was carried by the angels to Abraham's bosom* [in heaven]" (v. 22). So we see that a man can die practically in good health, but be lost, and a man can die with disease and be saved; so it is more important to be saved than anything else.

But Jesus was sent to bear the infirmities and the afflictions of the people, and to *"destroy the works of the devil"* (1 John 3:8). He said, *"The thief* [the Devil] *does not come except to steal, and to kill, and to destroy. I have come that they may have life, and that they may have it more abundantly"* (John 10:10). I maintain that God wishes all His people to have the more abundant life. We have the remedy for all sickness in the Word of God! Jesus paid the full price and the full redemption for every need, and where sin abounds, grace can come in and much more abound (Rom. 5:20), and dispel all the sickness.

When I was traveling by ship from England to Australia, I witnessed for Jesus, and it was not long before I had plenty of room to myself. If you want a whole seat to yourself, just begin to preach Jesus. However, some people listened and began to be much affected. One of the young men said to me, "I have never heard these truths before. You have so moved me that I must have a good conversation with you." The young man told me that his wife was a great believer in Christian Science, but that she was very sick now. Although she had tried everything, she had been unable to get relief, and so she was consulting a doctor. But the doctor gave her no hope whatsoever, and in her dilemma, and facing the reality of death, she asked that she might have an appointment with me.

When I went to see her in her cabin, I felt it would be unwise to say anything about Christian Science, so I said, "You are in bad shape." She said, "Yes, they give me no hope." I said, "I will not speak to you about anything, but will just lay my hands upon you in the name of Jesus, and when I do, you will be healed." That woke her up, and she began to think seriously. For three days, she was lamenting over the things she might have to give up. "Will I have to give up cigarettes?" "No," I said. "Will I have to give up dancing?" she asked. And again I replied, "No." "Well, we do a little drinking sometimes and then we play cards also. Will I have to give—." "No," I said, "you will not have to give up anything. Only let us see Jesus." And right then she got such a vision of her crucified Savior, and Jesus was made so real to her, that she at once told her friends that she could not play cards anymore, could not drink or dance anymore, and that she would have to go back to England to preach against this awful thing, Christian Science. Oh, what a revelation Jesus gave her! Now, if I had refused to go when called for, saying that I first had to go to my cabin and pray about it, the Lord might have let that opportunity slip by. After you have received the Holy Spirit, you have power; you don't have to wait.

The other day, we were going through a very thickly populated part of San Francisco when we noticed that a large crowd had gathered. I saw it from the window of the streetcar I was riding in, and I said that I had to get out, which I did. There in the midst of the crowd was a boy in the agonies of death. As I threw my arms around the boy, I asked what the trouble was, and he answered that he had cramps. In the name of Jesus, I commanded the devils to come out of him, and at once he jumped up and, not even taking time to thank me, ran off perfectly healed. We are God's own children, quickened by His Spirit, and He has given us power over all the powers of darkness (Luke 10:19). Christ in us is the open evidence of eternal glory. Christ in us is the Life, the Truth, and the Way (John 14:6).

THE GREATNESS OF THE POWER

We have a wonderful salvation that fits everybody. I believe that a person who is baptized in the Holy Spirit has no conception of the power God has given him until he uses what he has. I maintain that Peter and John had no idea of the greatness of the power they had, but they began to speculate. They said to the lame man who asked them for alms, "Well, as far as money goes, we have none of that, but we do have something; we don't exactly know what it is, but we will try it on you: *In the name of Jesus Christ of Nazareth, rise up and walk*" (Acts 3:6). And it worked. (See verses 1–10.)

In order to make yourself realize what you have in your possession, you will have to try it; and I can assure you, it will work all right. One time I said to a man that the Acts of the Apostles would never have been written if the apostles had not acted; and the Holy Spirit is still continuing His acts through us. May God help us to have some acts.

There is nothing like Pentecost, and if you have never been baptized in the Holy Spirit, you are making a big mistake by waiting. Don't you know that one of the main purposes for which God saved you was that you might bring salvation to others through Christ? For you to think that you have to remain stationary and just get to heaven is a great mistake. The baptism is to make you a witness for Jesus. The hardest way is the best way; you never hear anything about the person who is always having an easy time. The preachers always tell of how Moses crossed the Red Sea when he was at his wits' end. I cannot find a record of anyone in the Scriptures whom God used who was not first tried. So if you never have any trials, it is because you are not worth them.

God wants us to have power. When I was traveling on the train in Sweden early in the morning, a little lady and her daughter got onto the train at a certain station. I saw at once that the lady was in dreadful agony, and I asked my interpreter to inquire as to the trouble. With tears running down her face, she told how her daughter was taking her to the hospital to have her leg amputated. Everything possible had been done for her. I told her Jesus could heal. Just then the train stopped, and a crowd of people entered until there was hardly standing room; but friends, we never get into a place that is too awkward for God, though it seemed to me that the Devil had sent these people in at that time to hinder her healing. However, when the train began to move along, I got down, although it was terribly crowded, and, putting my hands upon the woman's leg, I prayed for her in the name of Jesus. At once, she said to her daughter, "I am healed. It is all different now; I felt the power go down my leg." And she began to walk around. Then the train stopped at the next station, and this woman got out and walked up and down the platform, saying, "I am healed. I am healed."

Jesus was the *"firstfruits"* (1 Cor. 15:20), and God has chosen us in Christ and has revealed His Son in us so that we might manifest Him in power. God gives us power over the Devil, and when I say the Devil, I mean everything that is not of God. Some people say we can afford to do without the baptism in the Spirit, but I say we cannot. I believe that any person who thinks there is a stop between Calvary and the glory has made a big mistake.

How to Be an Overcomer

In the first chapter of Mark, we read of John the Baptist, who, as we learn in Luke, was filled with the Holy Spirit *"from his mother's womb"* (Luke 1:15). Because of this mighty infilling, there was mighty message on his lips. (See Mark 1:1–4.) It was foretold of John by the prophet Isaiah that he would be *"the voice of one crying in the wilderness"* (Isa. 40:3). He was to lift up his voice with strength, and cry to the cities of Judah, *"Behold your God!"* (v. 9). And so we find John, as he pointed to Jesus at the Jordan River, crying out, *"Behold! The Lamb of God who takes away the sin of the world!"* (John 1:29). In this way, he proclaimed Jesus to be the One of whom Abraham prophesied when he said to his son Isaac in Genesis 22:8, *"God will provide for Himself the lamb"*—the Lamb of God and God the Lamb.

John was so filled with the Spirit of God that the cry he raised moved all Israel (Mark 1:5). This shows that when God gets hold of a person and fills him with the Spirit, he can have a cry, a message, a proclamation of the Gospel that will move people. A person who does not have the Spirit of the Lord may cry out for many years and not have anybody take notice of him. The person who is filled with the Spirit of God needs to cry out only once and people will feel the effect of it.

BE FILLED WITH THE SPIRIT OF GOD

This should teach us that there is a need for every one of us to be filled with the Spirit of God. It is not sufficient just to have a touch of God or to usually have a desire for God. There is only one thing that will meet the needs of the people today, and that is to be immersed in the life of God—God taking you and filling you with His Spirit, until you live right in God, and God lives in you, so that *"whether you eat or drink, or whatever you do,"* it will all be for the *"glory of God"* (1 Cor. 10:31). In that place, you will find that all your strength and all your mind and all your soul are filled with zeal, not only for worship, but to proclaim the Gospel message—a proclamation that is accompanied by the power of God (Rom. 1:16), which defeats satanic power, convicts the world, and contributes to the glory of God.

The reason the world is not seeing Jesus today is that *too many Christian people are not filled with the Spirit of Christ.* They are satisfied with going to church, occasionally reading the Bible, and sometimes praying. Beloved, if God lays hold of you by the Spirit, you will find that there is an end to everything of the old life. All the old things will have passed away, and all things will have become new—all things will be of God (2 Cor. 5:17–18). You will find that, as you are wholly yielded to God, your whole being will be transformed by the divine indwelling. He will take you in hand so that you may become *"a vessel for honor"* (2 Tim. 2:21).

Our lives are not to be for ourselves, for if we live for self, we will die. If we seek to save our lives, we will lose them, but if we lose our lives, we will save them (Matt. 16:25). If we, through the Spirit, *"put to death the deeds of the body"* (Rom. 8:13), we will live—live a life of freedom and joy and blessing and service, a life that will bring blessing to others. God wants us to see that we must *"be filled with the Spirit"* (Eph. 5:18), that we must every day *"live in the Spirit,...walk in the Spirit"* (Gal. 5:25), and be continually renewed in the Spirit.

Study the life of Jesus. It was quite a natural thing for Him, after He had served a whole day among the multitude, to want to go to His Father to pray all night. Why? He wanted a renewing of divine strength and power. He wanted fellowship with His Father. His Father would speak to Him the word that He was to bring to others, and would empower Him afresh for new ministry. He would come from those hours of sweet communion and fellowship with His Father clothed with His holy presence and Spirit, and, anointed with the Holy Spirit and power, He would go about doing good and healing all who were oppressed by the Enemy (Acts 10:38).

When He met sickness, it had to leave. He came from that holy time of communion with power to meet the needs of the people, whatever they were. It is an awful thing for me to see people who profess to be Christians but who are lifeless and powerless. The place of holy communion is open to us all. There is a place where we can be daily refreshed, renewed, and re-empowered.

In the fourth chapter of Hebrews, we are told, *"There remains therefore a rest for the people of God. For he who has entered His rest has himself also ceased from his works"* (vv. 9–10). Oh, what a blessed rest that is, to cease from your own works, to come to the place where God is now enthroned in your life, working in you day by day *"to will and to do for His good pleasure"* (Phil. 2:13), working in you an entirely new order of things.

God wants to bring you forth as a *"flame of fire"* (Heb. 1:7), with a message from God, with the truth that will defeat the powers of Satan, with an unlimited supply for every needy soul. So, just as John the Baptist moved all of Israel with a mighty cry, you too, by the power of the Holy Spirit, will move the people so that they repent and cry, *"What shall we do?"* (Luke 3:10, 12, 14).

BORN OF GOD

This is what Jesus meant when He said to Nicodemus,

> *Unless one is born again, he cannot see the kingdom of God....That which is born of the flesh is flesh, and that which is born of the Spirit is spirit. Do not marvel that I said to you, "You must be born again."*　　　(John 3:3, 6–7)

If we only knew what these words mean to us, to be born of God! They mean an infilling of the life of God, a new life from God, a new creation, living in the world but not of the world (John 17:11, 14), knowing the blessedness of this truth: *"Sin shall not have dominion over you"* (Rom. 6:14). How will we reach this place in the Spirit? By the provision that the Holy Spirit makes. If we live in the Spirit, we will find that all that is carnal in us is swallowed up in life. There is an infilling of the Spirit that gives life to our mortal bodies (Rom. 8:11).

Give God your life, and you will see that sickness has to go when God comes in fully. Then you are to walk before God, and you will find that He will perfect what concerns you. That is the place where He wants believers to live, the place where the Spirit of the Lord comes into your whole being. That is the place of victory.

Look at the disciples. Before they received the Holy Spirit, they were in bondage. When Christ said, *"One of you will betray Me"* (Matt. 26:21), they were all doubtful of themselves and asked, *"Lord, is it I?"* (v. 22). They were conscious of their human depravity and helplessness. Later, Peter said, *"Even if I have to die with You, I will not deny You!"* (v. 35). The others declared the same, yet they all forsook Him and fled when He was arrested. But after the power of God fell upon them in the Upper Room, they met difficulty like lions. They were bold. What made them so? The purity and power that is by the Spirit.

YOU CAN BE AN OVERCOMER

God can make you an overcomer. When the Spirit of God comes into your surrendered being, He transforms you. There is a life in the Spirit that makes you free, and there is an audacity about it, and there is a personality in it—it is God in you.

God is able to so transform you and change you that all the old order has to go before God's new order. Do you think that God will make you to be a failure?

God never made man to be a failure. He made man to be a son, to walk the earth in the power of the Spirit, to be master over the flesh and the Devil, until nothing arises within him except what will magnify and glorify the Lord.

Jesus came to set us free from sin, and to free us from sickness, so that we will go forth in the power of the Spirit and minister to the needy, sick, and afflicted. Through the revelation of the Word of God, we find that divine healing is solely for the glory of God, and that salvation is walking in newness of life so that we are inhabited by Another, even God.

Filled with God

For a short time, I want especially to speak to those of you who are saved. God wants us to bo holy. He wants us to be filled with a power that keeps us holy. He wants us to have a revelation of what sin and death are, and what the Spirit and the life of the Spirit are.

Look at the first two verses of Romans 8. They are full of meaning, sufficient to occupy us for two hours, but we must move on in order to help everybody. But look at these verses for a moment:

> *There is therefore now no condemnation to those who are in Christ Jesus, who do not walk according to the flesh, but according to the Spirit. For the law of the Spirit of life in Christ Jesus has made me free from the law of sin and death.* (Rom. 8:1–2)

"No condemnation." This is the primary phrase for me tonight because it means so much—it has everything within it. If you are without condemnation,

you are in a place where you can pray through, where you have a revelation of Christ. For Him to be in you brings you to a place where you cannot but follow the divine leadings of the Spirit of Christ, and where you have no fellowship with the world.

I want you to see that the Spirit of the Lord desires to reveal to us this fact: if you love the world (worldliness), you cannot love God, and the love of God cannot be in you (1 John 2:15). God wants a straight cut—a complete severing from worldliness. Why does God want a straight cut? Because if you are *"in Christ,"* you are a *"new creation"* (2 Cor. 5:17). You are in Him; you belong to a new creation in the Spirit, and therefore you *"walk in the Spirit"* (Gal. 5:16) and are free from condemnation.

THE LAW OF THE SPIRIT

So the Spirit of the Lord wants you without condemnation, and desires to bring you into revelation. Now, what will this mean? Much in every way, because God wants all His people to be targets, to be lights, to be like cities set on a hill that cannot be hidden (Matt. 5:14), to be so "in God" for the world's redemption that the world may know that they belong to God.

That is the law of the Spirit. What will it do? *"The law of the Spirit of life in Christ Jesus* [will make you] *free from the law of sin and death"* (Rom. 8:2). Sin will have no dominion over you (Rom. 6:14). You will have no desire to sin, and it will be as true in your case as it was in Jesus' when He said, "Satan comes, but finds nothing in Me." (See John 14:30.) Satan cannot condemn; he has no power. His power is destroyed. This fact is expressed in Romans 8:10. What does it say? *"The body is dead because of sin, but the Spirit is life because of righteousness."* To be filled with God means that you are free—full of joy, peace, blessing, power, and strength of character; molded afresh in God and transformed by His mighty power, until you *live.* Yet it is not you who live, but Another lives in you (Gal. 2:20), manifesting His power through you as sons of God.

Notice these two laws: *"The law of the Spirit of life in Christ Jesus* [makes you] *free from the law of sin and death"* (Rom. 8:2, emphasis added). The same *"law of sin and death"* is in you as was in you before, but it is dead. You are just the same person, only you have been made alive; it is the same flesh, but it is dead. You are a new creation, a new creature. You are created in God afresh according to the image of Christ.

Now, beloved, some people come into line with this, but they do not understand their inheritance in Christ, and therefore they are defeated. However, instead of being weak and being defeated, you have to rise triumphantly over *"the law of sin and death."* You say, "Show us *'the law of the Spirit of life in Christ Jesus.'"* I will, God helping me. It is found in Romans 7, the last verse: *"I thank God; through Jesus Christ our Lord! So then, with the mind I myself serve the law of God, but with the flesh the law of sin"* (v. 25).

Is it a sin to work? No, it is not a sin to work. Work is ordained by God. It is an honor to work. I find that there are two ways to work. One way is working in the flesh, but the child of God should never allow himself to come into the flesh when God has taken him in the Spirit. God wants to show you that there is a place where you can live in the Spirit and not be subject to the flesh. Live in the Spirit until sin has no dominion. *"Sin reigned in death"* (Rom. 5:21), but Christ reigns, and so we reign in Christ, over sin and death. (See verses 17–21.) Reigning in life.

THE GREATNESS OF REDEMPTION

There is not a person here who, if he is sick, is truly reigning in life. There is satanic power reigning there, but God wants you to know that you have to reign. God made you like Himself, and Jesus bought back for us in the Garden of Gethsemane everything that was lost in the Garden of Eden, and restored it to us through His agony. He bought that blessed redemption. When I think of redemption, I wonder if there is anything greater than the Garden of Eden, when Adam and Eve had fellowship with God, and He came down and walked with them in the cool of the evening (Gen. 3:8). Is there anything greater?

Yes, redemption is greater. How? Anything that is local is never as great. When God was in the Garden, Adam was local—within the boundaries of the Garden; but the moment a person is born again, he is free and lives in *"heavenly places"* (Eph. 1:3). He has no destination except the glory. Redemption is greater than the Garden, and God wants you to know that He wants you to come into this glorious redemption, not only for the salvation of your soul, but also for your body—to know that it is redeemed from *"the curse of the law"* (Gal. 3:13), to know that you have been set free, to know that God's Son has set you free. Hallelujah! *"Free from the law of sin and death"* (Rom. 8:2)! How is this accomplished? Romans 8:3–4 tell us. They are master verses:

> *For what the law could not do in that it was weak through the flesh, God did by sending*

154

His own Son in the likeness of sinful flesh, on account of sin: He condemned sin in the flesh, that the righteous requirement of the law might be fulfilled in us who do not walk according to the flesh but according to the Spirit.

Righteousness fulfilled in us! Brother! Sister! I tell you, there is a redemption, there is an atonement, in Christ—a personality of Christ to dwell in you. There is a Godlikeness for you to attain to—a blessed resemblance of Christ in you—if you will believe the Word of God. The Word is sufficient for you. Eat it; devour it. It is the living Word of God.

Jesus was manifested to *"destroy the works of the devil"* (1 John 3:8). God so manifested His fullness in Jesus that He walked this earth glorified and filled with God. In the first place, Jesus was with God from the beginning, and is called *"the Word"* (John 1:1). In the second place, He and God are united in their working, and the Bible says, *"The Word was God"* (v. 1).

The cooperation of oneness was so manifest that nothing was done without the Other. They cooperated in the working of power. You must understand that *"before the foundation of the world,"* this plan of redemption was completed (Eph. 1:4; 1 Pet. 1:20–21); it was set in order before the Fall. Notice that this redemption had to be so mighty, and to redeem us all so perfectly, that there would be no lack in the whole redemption. Let us see how it came about.

First, *"the Word became flesh"* (John 1:14); next He was filled with the Holy Spirit (Matt. 3:16); and then He became the voice and the operation of the Word by the power of God through the Holy Spirit. He became the Authority.

Let me go further. You are born of an incorruptible power—the power of God's Word—by His personality and His nature. (See 1 Peter 1:23.) You are *"born of God"* (1 John 5:18), and *"you are not your own"* (1 Cor. 6:19). Christ now lives in you, and you can believe that you have *"passed from death into life"* (John 5:24) and become an heir of God, a joint heir with Christ (Rom. 8:17), in the measure that you believe His Word. The natural flesh has been changed for a new order. The first order was the natural Adamic order; the last order is Christ—the heavenly order. (See 1 Corinthians 15:45–49.) And now you become changed by a heavenly power existing in your earthly body, a power that can never die; it can never *"see corruption"* (Acts 2:27), and it cannot be lost. If you are born of God, you are born of the power of the Word, and not of man. I want you to see that you are born of a power that exists within you, the power by which God made the world that you are in. It is *"the law of the Spirit of life in Christ Jesus* [that makes us] *free from the law of sin and death"* (Rom. 8:2). Did you accept it?

I want you all to see that what I have been preaching for two weeks in this place—divine life, divine healing, authority over satanic powers—is all biblical. If you will only believe it, you will be secure, for there is a power in you that is greater than in all the world (1 John 4:4). It is power over sin, power over death.

THE LAW OF SIN AND DEATH

Let us consider the contrast between two laws. First, let us look at the law without the Spirit—*"the law of sin and death"* (Rom. 8:2). Suppose there is a man here who has never known regeneration; he is led captive by the Devil at his will. There is no power that can convert men except the power of the blood of Jesus. Men try without it; science tries without it; all have tried without it; but all are left shaking on the brink of hell—without it. Nothing can deliver you but the blood of the Lamb. You can be free from the law of sin and death by the law of the Spirit of life in Christ Jesus. Then you will have clean hearts and pure lives.

Beloved, the carnal life is not subject to the will of God, nor indeed can it be (Rom. 8:7). Carnality is selfishness, uncleanness. It cannot be subject to God; it will not believe; it interferes with you; it binds you and keeps you in bondage. But, beloved, God destroys carnality. He destroys *the works of the flesh*" (Gal. 5:19). How? By a new life that is so much better, by a *"peace...which surpasses all understanding"* (Phil. 4:7), by a *"joy* [that is] *inexpressible and full of glory"* (1 Pet. 1:8).

OUR NEW LIFE IN GOD

This new life in God cannot be described. Everything that God does is too big to tell. His grace is too big. His love is too big. Why, it takes all heaven. His salvation is too big to be told; one cannot understand it. It is so vast, mighty, and wonderful—so "in God." But God gives us the power to understand it. Yes, of course, He does. Do you not know that ours is an abundant God? His love is far exceeding and abundant, above all that we can ask or think (Eph. 3:20).

Listen to this carefully! After you were illuminated, glory to God, you were quickened by the Spirit, and you are looking forward to a day of rapture, when you will be *"caught up"* and lifted into the presence of God (1 Thess. 4:17). You cannot think of God on any small line. God's lines have magnitude; they are wonderful, glorious. God can manifest them in our hearts with a greater fullness than we are able to express.

Let me address an important point. Christ Jesus has borne the cross for us—there is no need for us to bear it. He has borne the curse, for *"cursed is everyone who hangs on a tree"* (Gal. 3:13). The curse covered everything. The Word says that when Christ was in the grave, He was raised from the dead by the operation of God through the Spirit (Rom. 8:11). He was made alive in the grave by the Spirit, and the same Spirit that dwells in you will *"give life to your mortal bodies"* (v. 11). Jesus rose by the quickening power of the Holy Spirit, and

> *if the Spirit of Him who raised Jesus from the dead dwells in you, He who raised Christ from the dead will also give life to your mortal bodies through His Spirit who dwells in you.*
> (Rom. 8:11)

What does this mean? Right now, you do not have an immortal body. Immortality can only be obtained in the future resurrection. He will give life to your mortal bodies.

If you will allow Jesus to have control of your bodies, you will find that His Spirit will give you life, will loose you. He will show you that it is the mortal body that has to be given life. Talk about divine healing! You can't take it out of the Scriptures, for they are full of it. I see this. Everyone who is healed by the power of God—especially believers—will find their healing an incentive to make them purer and holier.

If divine healing was only to make you well, it would be worth nothing. Divine healing is a divine act of the providence of God coming into your mortal bodies and touching them with almightiness. Could you remain the same after being touched in this way? No. Like me, you would go out to worship and serve God. That is why I am here in Australia—because of the healing of God in my mortal body. I am not here to build new orders of things. I understand the fact that God wants me to preach so that everyone who hears me will go back to his own home with the energy and power of God and the revelation of Christ.

It is a fact that the more you are held in bondage and the more you shut your eyes to the truth, the more the Bible becomes a blank instead of life and joy. The moment you yield yourself to God, the Bible becomes a new Book; it becomes revelation, so that we have the fullness of redemption going right through our bodies in every way. Then we are filled with God, as Christ was filled with *"all the fullness of the God-head bodily"* (Col. 2:9).

> Filled with God! Yes, filled with God,
> Pardoned and cleansed, and filled with God.
> Filled with God! Yes, filled with God,
> Emptied of self, and filled with God!

The Power of Christ's Resurrection

That I may know Him and the power of His resurrection, and the fellowship of His sufferings, being conformed to His death, if, by any means, I may attain to the resurrection from the dead. Not that I have already attained, or am already perfected; but I press on, that I may lay hold of that for which Christ Jesus has also laid hold of me. Brethren, I do not count myself to have apprehended; but one thing I do, forgetting those things which are behind and reaching forward to those things which are ahead, I press toward the goal for the prize of the upward call of God in Christ Jesus.
—Philippians 3:10–14

What a wonderful Scripture passage! This surely means to press on to be filled with all the fullness of God. If we are not filled in this way, we will surely miss God, and we will fail in fulfilling the ministry He wants to give us.

The Lord wants us to preach by our lives and by our deeds, always abounding in service; to be living epistles, bringing forth to men the knowledge of God. If we went all the way with God, what would happen? What would we see if we would only seek to bring honor to the name of our God? In this passage from Philippians, we see Paul pressing in for this purpose. There is no standing still. We must move on to a fuller power of the Spirit, never satisfied that we have attained all, but filled with the assurance that God will take us on to the goal we desire to reach, as we press on for the prize ahead.

Abraham came out from Ur of the Chaldeans (Gen. 11:31). We never get into a new place until we come out from the old one. There is a place where we leave the old life behind, and where the life in Christ fills us and we are filled with His glorious personality.

On the road to Damascus, Saul of Tarsus was apprehended by Christ. (See Acts 9:1–6.) From the first, he sent up the cry, *"Lord, what do You want me to do?"* (v. 6). He always desired to do the will of God, but we see in this passage, which he wrote to the Philippian believers, that he longed for a place of closer intimacy, a place of fuller power, of deeper crucifixion. He saw a prize ahead, and every fiber of his being was intent on securing that prize.

Jesus Christ came to be the *"firstfruits"* (1 Cor. 15:20)—the firstfruits of a great harvest of fruit like Himself. How zealous the farmer is as he watches his crops and sees the first shoots and blades. They are the pledge of the great harvest that is coming. In the passage from Philippians, Paul longed that the Father's heart would be satisfied, for in that first resurrection (Rev. 20:6), the Heavenly Husbandman will see a firstfruit harvest—a harvest of firstfruits that are like Christ, sons of God made conformable to the only begotten Son of God.

GOD DELIGHTS TO WORK IN DIFFICULT SITUATIONS

You say, "I am in a needy place." It is in the needy places that God delights to work. One time, when a great multitude of people came to Jesus for healing, it grew late in the day, and Christ asked Philip, *"Where shall we buy bread, that these may eat?"* (John 6:5). That was a hard place for Philip, but not for Jesus, for He knew exactly what He would do. The hard place is where He delights to show forth His miraculous power. And how fully was the need provided for! There was food enough for five thousand, and more to spare! (See John 6:7–13.)

Two troubled, baffled travelers were on the road to Emmaus after the crucifixion of Jesus. As they communed together and reasoned, Jesus Himself drew near, and He opened up the Word to them in such a way that they saw light in His light. Their eyes were prevented from recognizing the One who was talking with them. But oh, how their hearts burned within as He opened up the Scriptures to them. And at the breaking of bread, He was made known to them. (See Luke 24:13–35.) Always seek to be found in the place where He manifests His presence and power.

The resurrected Christ appeared to Peter and several of the other disciples early one morning on the shore of the Sea of Galilee. He prepared a meal for the tired, tried disciples. (See John 21:1–13.) That is just like Him. Count on His presence. Count on His power.

Count on His provision. He is always there just where you need Him.

Have you received Him? Are you to be *"found in Him"* (Phil. 3:9)? Have you received His righteousness, which is by faith? Abraham got to this place, for God gave His righteousness to him because he believed (Rom. 4:3); and as you believe God, He credits His righteousness to your account. He will put His righteousness within you. He will keep you in perfect peace as you fix your mind upon Him and trust in Him (Isa. 26:3). He will bring you to a rest of faith, to a place of blessed assurance that all that happens is working for your eternal good (Rom. 8:28).

COMPASSION IS GREATER THAN SUFFERING

The Bible tells us about a widow from the town of Nain whose son had died; she was taking him to be buried. (See Luke 7:11–17.) Jesus met that sad funeral procession. He had compassion on that poor woman who was taking her only son to the cemetery. His great heart had such compassion that death had no power—it could no longer hold its prey. Compassion is greater than suffering. Compassion is greater than death. Oh God, give us compassion! In His infinite compassion, Jesus stopped that funeral procession and cried to the widow's son, *"Young man, I say to you, arise"* (v. 14). And he who was dead sat up, and Jesus presented him to his mother.

Paul had a vision and revelation of the resurrection power of Christ, and so, in the passage from Philippians, he was saying, "I will not stop until I have laid hold of what God has laid hold of me for." (See Philippians 3:12.) For what purpose has God laid hold of us? To be channels for His power. He wants to manifest the power of the Son of God through you and me. May God help us to manifest the faith of Christ, the compassion of Christ, the resurrection power of Christ.

One morning, about eleven o'clock, I visited a woman who was suffering from a tumor. She could not live through the day. A little blind girl led me to her bedside. Compassion broke me up, and I wanted that woman to live for the child's sake. I said to the woman, "Do you want to live?" She could not speak. She just moved her finger. I anointed her with oil and said, "In the name of Jesus." There was a stillness of death that followed; and the pastor, looking at the woman, said to me, "She is gone."

When God pours in His compassion, it has resurrection power in it. I carried that woman across the room, put her against a wardrobe, and held her there. I said, "In the name of Jesus, Death, come out." And soon her body began to tremble like a leaf. "In Jesus' name, walk," I said. She did, and then she went back to bed.

I told this story in the assembly. There was a doctor there, and he said, "I'll prove that." He went to the woman, and she told him it was perfectly true. She said, "I was in heaven, and I saw countless numbers, all like Jesus. Then I heard a voice saying, 'Walk, in the name of Jesus.'"

There is power in the name of Jesus. Let us take hold of the power of His resurrection, the power of His compassion, the power of His love. Love will break the hardest thing—there is nothing it will not break.

Men of Faith:
The Life That Ventures on the Word of God

God has drawn us together, and He has something to give us. He is not ordinary, but extraordinary; not measured, but immeasurable, abounding in everything. There is nothing small about our God, and when we understand God, we will find out that there should not be anything small about us. We must have an enlargement of our conception of God. Then we will know that we have come to a place where all things are possible, for our God is an omnipotent God for impossible situations.

We are born into a family that never dies, and it is the plan of God to subdue all things that are natural to a supernatural order. Nothing about us has to be dwarfed. God comes in with His mighty power and so works in us that sin has no dominion (Rom. 6:14); evil is subdued, and God's Son begins to reign on the throne of your heart, transforming what was weak and helpless.

But there must be a revolution if we want the almighty God living in and controlling our mortal flesh. We must conclude that there is no good thing in the flesh (Rom. 7:18), and then we must know that God can come into the flesh and subject it until every mighty thing can be manifested through the human order.

Now, beloved, have you come for a blessing? Turn to Hebrews, chapter eleven.

The Christian life continues nonstop until you reach heaven. We must keep going on. If you ever stop between Calvary and the glory, it is you who blocked the way. There is no stop between Calvary and the glory except by human failure; but if we allow God to have His way, He will surely transform us, for His plan is to change us from what we are to what He intends us to be, and never to lose the ideal of His great plan for us. God wants to shake us loose and take the cobwebs away, and to remove all the husks from the wheat, so that we may be pure grain for God to work upon. In order for Him to do that, we must be willing to let go; as long as you hold onto the natural, you cannot take hold of divine life.

VENTURE THE IMPOSSIBLE

The child of God never has to speculate; he only has to have faith, with audacity to prove that God is what He has promised to be. You will not become strong in faith until you venture the impossible.

If you ask for anything six times, five of the times are unbelief. You are not heard for your *"many words"* (Matt. 6:7), but because you believe. If you pray around the world, you will get into a whirlwind, and spoil every meeting you get into.

Now God does not want anybody in the world, under any circumstances, to be in a place where he lives on eyesight and on feelings. Faith never looks and faith never feels. Faith is an act, and faith without an act is not faith, but doubt and disgrace. Every one of you has more faith than you are using.

Now this *"substance"* (Heb. 11:1) that I am speaking about cannot be looked at or handled. God wants us to have something greater than what we can see and handle. It is declared in the Scriptures that the earth is going to be melted with fervent heat and the heavens will depart (2 Pet. 3:10, 12), but this Word will remain (Matt. 24:35), and this is substance. So we must know whether we are living in substance that cannot be handled or living in the temporal, for everything you can see is going to be removed, and what you cannot see is going to remain forever.

God gives us this remarkable substance that is called faith. It consists of the Word of God, the personality of God, the nature of God, and the acts of God, and these four things are all in faith. Faith is a deep reality caused by God's personality waking up our humanity to leap into eternal things and be lost forever in something a million times greater than ourselves—to be possessed by and be the possessor of something a million times greater than ourselves!

Go On with God

There is a growing in faith after we are saved. Backsliding is knowing the way of holiness but shutting the door. So if you know to do good and you do not do it, that is backsliding (James 4:17). What standard is holiness? There is none. A person who is newborn in Christ is as holy as the aged believer while he walks according to the light he has, and the oldest saint with more light is not more holy than the person who has just been saved and is walking in the light.

You cannot make anything without material, but I want to read to you of something being made without material: *"By faith we understand that the worlds were framed by the word of God, so that the things which are seen were not made of things which are visible"* (Heb. 11:3).

God took the Word and made this world out of things that were not there. He caused it all to come by the word of faith. You were born of, created by, made anew by the same Word that made the world. God, in His infinite mercy, brings His infinite light and power right into our finite beings so that we have revelations of the mighty God and of His wonderful power. That is the reason why I lay hands on the sick and know they will be healed.

God has included all ranks and conditions of people in the eleventh chapter of Hebrews. Samson made terrible mistakes, but he is included. Then there is Barak, who wouldn't go without Deborah. He couldn't have been a strong man if a woman had to go with him, but he is mentioned. Now why can you not believe that God will also include you?

The Acts of the Apostles finishes abruptly. It is not complete, and all who are in this place tonight must add to the Acts of the Apostles. It is an incomplete record, because when you get there, you will find that you are among the Acts of the Apostles.

LET NOBODY TAKE YOUR CROWN

You have to be zealous. You must not let anybody stand in your way. Salvation is the beginning;

sanctification is a continuation; the baptism in the Holy Spirit is the enlargement of capacity for the risen Christ. God comes along and inspires your thoughts, and says, "Now, go forward, my child; it will be all right. Do not give in."

The Lord may permit your tire to be punctured many times, but you must not be discouraged that the air has gone out. You must pump it up again. The life that He began cannot be taken away from you. If you have an inspiration to "go forth," you cannot be stopped. You know you are called to an eternal purpose, and nothing will stand in your way. It is His purpose that we will be sanctified, purified, and renewed. We are a people who have been raised from the dead, and if Jesus comes, you will go to be with Him because you have resurrection in you.

When our forefathers had a good report, it was always because of faith, and if devastating winds blow, it does not matter.

RELYING ON THE THINGS THAT ARE NOT

Men of faith are not moved by anything they see or hear. The man of faith does not live in time. He has begun in eternity. He does not count on the things that are; he relies on the things that are not.

We must be in the place of buoyancy. The man of faith is subject to God, but never in subjection to the Devil. He is not puffed up. No, he lives in meekness and grows in grace. If you ask God to give you power, you have fallen from grace. You *have* power after the Holy Spirit has come upon you (Acts 1:8). Act in faith. Act in wisdom, *"for it is God who works in you both to will and to do for His good pleasure"* (Phil. 2:13).

The Power of the Gospel

I am convinced that there is nothing in the world that is going to persuade men and women of the power of the Gospel like the manifestation of the Spirit with the fruits. God has baptized us in the Holy Spirit for a purpose: that He may show His mighty power in human flesh, as He did in Jesus. He is bringing us to a place where He may manifest these gifts.

JESUS IS THE WORD

"No one speaking by the Spirit of God calls Jesus accursed, and no one can say that Jesus is Lord except by the Holy Spirit" (1 Cor. 12:3). Everyone who does not speak the truth concerning this Word, which is Jesus, makes Him the accursed; so all we have to do is to have the revelation of the Word in our hearts, and there will be no fear of our being led astray, because this Word is nothing else but Jesus.

In the gospel of John, we read that *"the Word was God"* (1:1), and that He *"became flesh and dwelt among us, and we beheld His glory, the glory as of the only begotten* [Son] *of the Father"* (v. 14). So it is revealed that He is the Son of God—the Word of God. The Bible is nothing else than the Word of God, and you can know right away—without getting mixed up at all—that everything that does not confess it is not of the Holy Spirit, and consequently you can wipe out all such things. There is no difficulty about saving yourselves, because the Word of God will always save.

WE RECEIVE THE ANOINTING OF THE HOLY ONE

There are diversities of gifts, but the same Spirit. There are differences of ministries, but the same Lord. And there are diversities of activities, but it is the same God who works all in all. But the manifestation of the Spirit is given to each one for the profit of all. (1 Cor. 12:4–7)

My heart is in this business. I am brought face-to-face with the fact that now the Holy Spirit is dwelling within me, that He is dwelling in my body; as John said, the anointing of the Holy One is within (1 John 2:20). The anointing of the Holy One is the Holy Spirit manifested in us. So we see that right away, within us, there is the power to manifest and bring forth those gifts that He has promised; and these gifts will be manifested in the measure that we live in the anointing of the Spirit of God. Thus we will find out that those gifts must be manifested.

My brother here, Mr. Moser, was suffering from lack of sleep. He had not had a full night of sleep for

174

a long time. Last night I said, "I command you, in the
name of Jesus, to sleep." When he came this morning,
he was well; he had had a good night's sleep.

THE GIFTS ARE FOR THE PROFIT OF ALL

Beloved, the power of the Holy Spirit is within us
"for the profit of all" (1 Cor. 12:7). The Holy Spirit says
in the Scriptures,

> *To one is given the word of wisdom through
> the Spirit, to another the word of knowledge
> through the same Spirit, to another faith by the
> same Spirit, to another gifts of healings by the
> same Spirit, to another the working of miracles,
> to another prophecy, to another discerning of
> spirits, to another different kinds of tongues, to
> another the interpretation of tongues. But one
> and the same Spirit works all these things, dis-
> tributing to each one individually as He wills.*
> (1 Cor. 12:8–11)

Paul distinctly said that it is possible for a person
not to *"come short"* (1 Cor. 1:7) in any gift, according
to the measure of faith that he receives from the Lord
Jesus. (See verses 4–9.) No doubt, some of you have
sometimes thought what a blessed thing it would be
if you had been the Virgin Mary. Listen, a certain
woman said to Jesus, *"Blessed is the womb that bore
You, and the breasts which nursed You!"* (Luke 11:27).
But He answered, *"More than that, blessed are those –
who hear the word of God and keep it!"* (v. 28).

You see that a higher position than Mary's is
attained through simple faith in what the Scriptures
say. If we receive the Word of God as it is given to us,

there will be power in our bodies to claim the gifts of God, and it will amaze the world when they see the power of God manifested through these gifts.

I believe that we are coming to a time when these gifts will be more distinctly manifested. What can be more convincing? Yes, He is a lovely Jesus. He went forth from place to place, rebuking demons, healing the sick, and doing other wonderful things. What was the reason? *"God was with Him"* (Acts 10:38).

Wherever there is a child of God who dares to receive the Word of God and cherish it, there God is made manifest in the flesh, for the Word of God is life and spirit (John 6:63), and brings us into a place where we know that we have power with God and with men, in proportion to our loyalty of faith in the Word of God.

Now, beloved, I feel somehow that we have missed the greatest principle that underlies the baptism in the Holy Spirit. The greatest principle is that God the Holy Spirit came into our bodies to manifest the mighty works of God, *"for the profit of all"* (1 Cor. 12:7). He does not manifest only one gift, but as God the Holy Spirit abides in my body, I find that He fills it, and then one can truly say that it is the anointing of the Holy One. It so fills us that we feel we can command demons to come out of those who are possessed; and when I lay hands on the sick in the name of the Lord Jesus, I realize that my body is merely the outer coil, and that within is the Son of God. For I receive the word of Christ, and Christ is in me, the power of God is in me. The Holy Spirit is making that word a living word, and the Holy Spirit makes me say, "Come out!" It is not Wigglesworth. It is the power of the Holy Spirit that manifests the glorious presence of Christ.

The Gift of Tongues

*Pursue love, and desire spiritual gifts, but especially
that you may prophesy. For he who speaks in a ["an
unknown," KJV] tongue does not speak to men but to
God, for no one understands him; however,
in the spirit he speaks mysteries.*
—1 Corinthians 14:1–2

t is necessary that we have a great desire for spiritual gifts. We must thirst after them and covet them earnestly because the gifts are necessary and important, and so that we, having received the gifts by the grace of God, may be used for God's glory.

Tongues Are for Intercession

God has ordained this speaking in an unknown tongue to Himself as a wonderful, supernatural means of communication in the Spirit. As we speak to Him in an unknown tongue, we speak wonderful mysteries in the Spirit. In Romans 8:27, we read, *"He who searches the hearts knows what the mind of the Spirit*

177

is, because He makes intercession for the saints according to the will of God." Many times, as we speak to God in an unknown tongue, we are in intercession; and as we pray thus in the Spirit, we pray according to the will of God. And there is such a thing as the Spirit making intercession *"with groanings which cannot be uttered"* (v. 26).

Along these lines, I want to tell you about Willie Burton, who is laboring for God in the Belgium Congo (Zaire). Brother Burton is a mighty man of God and is giving his life for the heathen in Africa. At one point, he took fever and went down to death. Those who ministered with him said, "He has preached his last. What shall we do?" All their hopes seemed to be blighted, and there they stood, with broken hearts, wondering what was going to take place. They had left him for dead; however, in a moment, without any signal, he stood right in the midst of them, and they could not understand it. The explanation he gave was that when he came to himself, he felt a warmth going right through his body, and there wasn't one thing wrong with him.

How did this happen? It was a mystery until he went to London and was telling the people how he had been left for dead and then was raised up. A lady came up and asked for a private conversation with him, and they arranged a time to meet. When they met together, she asked, "Do you keep a diary?" He answered, "Yes." Then she told him, "It happened that, on a certain day, I went to pray; and as soon as I knelt, I had you on my mind. The Spirit of the Lord took hold of me and prayed through me in an unknown tongue. A vision came before me in which I saw you lying helpless; and I cried out in the unknown tongue until I saw you rise up and go out of that room." She had kept a note of the time, and when he looked in his diary, he found that it was exactly the time when he was raised up. There are great possibilities as we yield to the Spirit and speak to God in quiet hours in our bedrooms. God wants you to be filled with the Holy Spirit so that everything about you will be charged with the dynamite of heaven.

TONGUES ARE FOR PERSONAL EDIFICATION

"He who speaks in a tongue edifies himself, but he who prophesies edifies the church" (1 Cor. 14:4). I want you to see that he who speaks in an unknown tongue edifies himself, or builds himself up. We must be edified before we can edify the church. I cannot estimate what I, personally, owe to the Holy Spirit method of spiritual edification. I am here before you as one of the biggest conundrums in the world. There never was a weaker man on the platform. Did I have the capacity to speak? Not at all. I was full of inability. All natural things in my life point to exactly the opposite of my being able to stand on the platform and preach the Gospel. The secret is that the Holy Spirit came and brought this wonderful edification of the Spirit. I had been reading the Word continually as well as I could, but the Holy Spirit came and took hold of it, for the Holy Spirit is the breath of it, and He illuminated it to me. He gives me a spiritual language that I cannot speak fast enough; it comes too fast; and it is there because God has given it. When the Comforter, or Helper, comes, *"He will teach you **all** things"* (John 14:26, emphasis added); and He has given me this supernatural means of speaking in an unknown

tongue to edify myself, so that, after being edified, I can edify the church.

THE ANOINTING REMAINS IN YOU

In 1 John 2:20, we read, *"But you have an anointing from the Holy One, and you know all things."* Then, in verse 27, we read,

> But the anointing which you have received from Him abides in you, and you do not need that anyone teach you; but as the same anointing teaches you concerning all things, and is true, and is not a lie, and just as it has taught you, you will abide in Him.

Even when you are baptized in the Spirit, you may say, "I seem so dry; I don't know where I am." The Word says you have an anointing. Thank God you have received an anointing. In the above passage, the Holy Spirit says that He *"abides"* and that He *"teaches you concerning all things."* These are great and definite positions for you. The Holy Spirit wants you to stir up your faith to believe that this word is true—that you have the anointing and that the anointing abides. As you rise up in the morning, believe this wonderful truth; and as you yield to the Spirit's presence and power, you will find yourself speaking to God in the Spirit, and you will find that you are personally being edified by doing this. Let everything about you be a lie, but let this word of God be true. The Devil will say that you are the driest person and that you will never do anything; but believe God's word, that *"the anointing which you have received from Him abides in you."*

PROPHECY AND THE INTERPRETATION OF TONGUES

I wish you all spoke with tongues, but even more that you prophesied; for he who prophesies is greater than he who speaks with tongues, unless indeed he interprets, that the church may receive edification. (1 Cor. 14:5)

You must understand that God wants you to be continually in the place of prophecy, for everyone who has received the Holy Spirit has a right to prophesy. In 1 Corinthians 14:31, we read, *"You can all prophesy one by one."* Now prophecy is far in advance of speaking in tongues, except when you have the interpretation of the speaking in tongues, and then God gives an equivalent to prophecy. In verse 13, we read, *"Let him who speaks in a tongue pray that he may interpret."* This is an important word.

TWO TYPES OF TONGUES

After I received the baptism in the Holy Spirit and spoke in tongues as the Spirit gave utterance (Acts 2:4), I did not speak in tongues again for nine months. I was troubled about it because I went up and down laying hands upon people so that they might receive the Holy Spirit, and they were speaking in tongues, but I did not have the joy of speaking in them myself. God wanted to show me that the speaking in tongues as the Spirit gave utterance, which I received when I received the baptism, was distinct from the gift of tongues that I subsequently received. When I laid hands on other people and they received the Holy Spirit, I used to think, "Oh, Lord Jesus, it would

181

be nice if You would let me speak in tongues." He withheld the gift from me, for He knew that I would meet many who would say that the baptism of the Holy Spirit can be received without the speaking in tongues, and that people simply received the gift of tongues when they received the baptism.

I did not receive the gift of tongues when I received the baptism; however, nine months later, I was going out the door one morning, speaking to the Lord in my own heart, when a flood of tongues poured forth from me. When the tongues stopped, I said to the Lord, "Now, Lord, I did not do it, and I wasn't seeking it; therefore, You have done it, and I am not going to move from this place until you give me the interpretation." And then came an interpretation that has been fulfilled all over the world. Is it not the Holy Spirit who speaks? Then the Holy Spirit can interpret. Let him who speaks in a tongue ask for the interpretation, and God will give it. We must not rush through without getting a clear understanding of what God has to say to us.

Praying with the Spirit and with the Understanding

"What is the conclusion then? I will pray with the spirit, and I will also pray with the understanding. I will sing with the spirit, and I will also sing with the understanding" (1 Cor. 14:15). If you pray in an unknown tongue in the Spirit, you do not know what you are praying; you have no understanding of it; it is unfruitful to those around you. But you have the same power to pray with the understanding under the anointing of the Spirit as you have to pray in an unknown tongue.

182

Some say, "Oh, I could do that, but it would be myself doing it." If *you* pray, it is yourself, and everything you do in the beginning is yourself. When I kneel down to pray, the first and second sentences may be in the natural; but as soon as *I* have finished, the Spirit begins to pray through me. Granted, the first may be yourself. The next will be the Holy Spirit, and the Holy Spirit will take you through, praise the Lord. Everything but faith will say, "That isn't right." Faith says, "It is right." The natural man says, "It isn't right." Faith says, "It is right." Paul said, *"I will pray with the spirit, and I will also pray with the understanding"* (1 Cor. 14:15), and he did it in faith.

The Devil is against it, and your own self-life is against it. May God the Holy Spirit bring us into that blessed place where we may live, walk, pray, and sing in the Spirit, and pray and sing with the understanding, also. Faith will do it. Faith has a deaf ear to the Devil and to the working of the natural mind, and a big ear to God. Faith has a deaf ear to yourself and an open ear to God. Faith won't take any notice of feelings. Faith says, *"You are complete in Him"* (Col. 2:10).

It is a wonderful thing to pray in the Spirit and to sing in the Spirit—praying in tongues and singing in tongues as the Spirit of God gives you utterance. I never get out of bed in the morning without having communion with God in the Spirit. It is the most wonderful thing on earth. It is most lovely to be in the Spirit when you are getting dressed, and then when you come out into the world, to find that the world has no effect on you. If you begin the day like that, you will be conscious of the guidance of the Spirit all during the day.

TONGUES SHOULD BE SPOKEN IN AN ORDERLY WAY

I thank my God I speak with tongues more than you all; yet in the church I would rather speak five words with my understanding, that I may teach others also, than ten thousand words in a ["an unknown," KJV] tongue. (1 Cor. 14:18–19)

Many people will come to you and declare that Paul said he would rather speak five words with the known tongue than ten thousand words without understanding. They will always leave out the part of the passage that reads, *"I thank my God I speak with tongues more than you all"* (1 Cor. 14:18). In this passage, Paul was correcting the practice of excessive speaking in tongues without interpretation, which would not edify the assembly. If there was no one with the gift of interpretation present, the people were simply to speak to themselves and to God.

Suppose someone was preaching and twenty or thirty people stood up in succession to speak in tongues. It would be a very serious problem. There would be confusion. The people attending the meeting would rather have five words of edification, consolation, and comfort (1 Cor. 14:3) than ten thousand words without understanding.

Just because you feel a touch of the Spirit, you are not obligated to speak in tongues. The Lord will give you a sound mind (2 Tim. 1:7), so that you will hold your body in perfect order for the edification of the church. But in 1 Corinthians 14:18, Paul said that he spoke in tongues more than all of the Corinthians; and, as it is evident that the Corinthian church was very considerably given to speaking in tongues, he certainly must have been speaking in tongues a great amount both day and night. He was so edified by this wonderful, supernatural means of being built up, that he could go to the church preaching in a manner in which they could all understand him, and could marvelously edify the believers.

SEEK GOD'S BEST WITH ALL YOUR HEART

I will explain to you the most perfect way to receive the gift. Come with me to the second chapter of 2 Kings and I will show you a man receiving a gift. The prophet Elijah had been mightily used by God in calling down fire and in other miracles. Elisha, his chosen successor, was moved with a great spirit of covetousness to have this man's gifts. You can be very covetous for the gifts of the Spirit and God will allow it. When Elijah said to him, "I want you to stay at Gilgal," Elisha said, *"As the LORD lives, and as your soul lives, I will not leave you!"* (2 Kings 2:1–2). There was no stopping him. Likewise, when Elijah wanted Elisha to stay at Jericho, he said, in essence, "I am not stopping." The man who stops gets nothing. Oh, don't stop at Jericho; don't stop at Jordan; don't stop anywhere when God wants you to move on into all of His fullness that He has for you.

Elijah and Elisha came to the Jordan River, and Elijah took his mantle and struck the waters. The waters divided, and Elijah and Elisha went across on dry ground. Elijah turned to Elisha and said, in essence, "Look here, what do you want?" Elisha wanted what he was going to have, and you may covet all that God says that you shall have. Elisha said, *"Please let a double portion of your spirit be upon me"* (2 Kings 2:9). This was the plowboy who had washed the hands of his master (1 Kings 19:19–20; 2 Kings 3:11); but his spirit got so big that he purposed in his heart that, when Elijah stepped off the scene, he would be put into his place.

Elijah said, *"You have asked a hard thing. Nevertheless, if you see me when I am taken from you, it shall be so for you"* (2 Kings 2:10). May God help you never to stop persevering until you get what you want. Let your aspiration be large and your faith rise until you are wholly on fire for God's best.

Onward they went, and as one stepped, the other stepped with him. Elisha purposed to keep his eyes on his master until the last. It took a chariot of fire and horses of fire to separate them, and Elijah went up by a whirlwind into heaven. I can imagine Elisha crying out, "Father Elijah, drop that mantle." And it came down. Oh, I can see it lowering and lowering and lowering. Elisha took all of his own clothes and tore them in two pieces, and then he took up the mantle of Elijah. (See verses 11–13.) I do not believe that, when he put on that other mantle, he felt any different in himself; but when he came to the Jordan, he took the mantle of Elijah, struck the waters, and said, *"Where is the LORD God of Elijah?"* (v. 14). The waters parted, and he went over on dry ground. And the sons of the prophets said, *"The spirit of Elijah rests on Elisha"* (v. 15).

It is like receiving a gift; you don't know that you have it until you act in faith. Brothers and sisters, as you ask, *believe.*

The Gift of Prophecy

In 1 Corinthians 12:10, speaking of the diversities of gifts given by the same Spirit (v. 4), Paul wrote, *"To another [is given] prophecy."* We see the importance of this gift from 1 Corinthians 14:1, where we are told to *"pursue love, and desire spiritual gifts, but especially that you may prophesy."* We also see that *"he who prophesies speaks edification and exhortation and comfort to men"* (v. 3). How important it is, then, that we should have this gift in manifestation in the church, so that believers might be built up and made strong and filled with the comfort of God. But with this, as with all other gifts, we should see that it is operated by the Spirit's power and brought forth in the anointing of the Spirit, so that everyone who hears prophecy—as it is brought forth by the Spirit of God—will know that it is truly God who is bringing forth what is for the edification of those who hear. It is the Spirit of God who takes of the *"deep things of God"* (1 Cor. 2:10) and reveals them, and anoints the prophet to give forth what is a revelation of the things of God.

Utterance in prophecy has a real lifting power and sheds real light on the truth to those who hear. Prophecy is never a reflection of our minds; it is something far deeper than this. By means of prophecy, we receive what is the mind of the Lord; and as we receive these blessed, fresh utterances through the Spirit of the Lord, the whole assembly is lifted into the realm of the spiritual. Our hearts and minds and whole bodies receive a quickening through the Spirit-given word. As the Spirit brings forth prophecy, we find there is healing, salvation, and power in every sentence. For this reason, it is one of the gifts that we ought to covet.

FALSE VERSUS TRUE PROPHECY

While we appreciate true prophecy, we must not forget that the Scriptures warn us in no uncertain terms concerning what is false. In 1 John 4:1, we are told, *"Beloved, do not believe every spirit, but test the spirits, whether they are of God; because many false prophets have gone out into the world."* John then went on to tell us how we can tell the difference between the true and the false:

> *By this you know the Spirit of God: Every spirit that confesses that Jesus Christ has come in the flesh is of God, and every spirit that does not confess that Jesus Christ has come in the flesh is not of God. And this is the spirit of the Antichrist, which you have heard was coming, and is now already in the world.* (1 John 4:2–3)

There are voices that seem like prophecy, and some believers have fallen into terrible darkness and bondage through listening to these counterfeits of the true gift of prophecy. True prophecy is always Christ exalting, magnifying the Son of God, exalting the blood of Jesus Christ, encouraging believers to praise and worship the true God. False prophecy deals with things that do not edify and is designed to puff up its hearers and to lead them into error.

Many people picture Satan as a great, ugly monster with large ears, eyes, and a tail; but the Scriptures give us no such picture of him. He was a being of great beauty, but his heart became lifted up against God. He is manifesting himself everywhere today as an *"angel of light"* (2 Cor. 11:14). He is full of pride, and if you aren't careful, he will try to make you think you are somebody. This is the weakness of most preachers and most men—the idea of being somebody! None of us are anything, and the more we know we are nothing, the more God can make us a channel of His power. May the dear Lord save us from continually being sidetracked by pride—it is the Devil's trap. True prophecy will show you that Christ is *"all in all"* (Eph. 1:23), and that you are, in yourself, less than nothing and vanity. False prophecy will not magnify Christ, but will make you think that you are going to be someone great after all. You may be sure that such thoughts are inspired by "the chief of the sons of pride."

I want to warn you against the foolishness of continually seeking to hear "voices." Look in the Bible. There we have the voice of God, *"who at various times and in various ways spoke in time past to the fathers by the prophets, [and] has in these last days spoken to us by His Son"* (Heb. 1:1–2). Don't run away with anything else. If you hear the voice of God, it will be according to the Scriptures of Truth given in the inspired Word. In Revelation 22:18–19, we see the danger of attempting to add to or take from the prophecy of this Book. True prophecy, as it comes forth in the power of the Spirit of God, will neither take from nor add to the Scriptures, but will intensify and quicken what already has been given to us by God. The Holy Spirit will bring to our remembrance all the things that Jesus said and did (John 14:26). True prophecy will bring forth *"things new and old"* (Matt. 13:52) out of the Scriptures of Truth and will make them *"living and powerful"* (Heb. 4:12) to us.

Some may ask, "If we have the Scriptures, why do we need prophecy?" The Scriptures themselves answer this question. God has said that in the last days He will pour out His Spirit upon all flesh, and that *"your sons and your daughters shall prophesy"* (Acts 2:17). The Lord knew that, in these last days, prophecy would be a real means of blessing to us, and that is why we can count on Him to give us, by means of the Spirit, through His menservants and His maidservants, true prophetic messages (v. 18).

THE DANGERS OF LISTENING TO FALSE VOICES

Again, I want to warn you concerning listening to voices. I was at a meeting in Paisley, Scotland, and I came in touch with two young women. They were in a great state of excitement. These two girls were telegraph operators and were precious young women, having received the baptism in the Spirit. They were both longing to be missionaries. But whatever our spiritual state is, we are subject to temptations. An evil power came to one of these young women and said, "If you will obey me, I will make you one of the most wonderful missionaries who ever went out to the mission field." This was just the Devil or one of his agents acting as an angel of light. The young women was captured immediately by this suggestion, and she became so excited that her sister saw there was something wrong and asked their work supervisor if they could be excused for a while.

As the sister took her into a room, the power of Satan, endeavoring to imitate the Spirit of God, manifested itself in a voice, and led this young woman to believe that the missionary enterprise would be unfolded that night, if she would obey. This evil spirit said, "Don't tell anybody but your sister." I think that everything of God can be told to everybody. If you cannot preach what you live, your life is wrong. If you are afraid of telling what you do in secret, some day it will be told from the housetops (Luke 12:3). Don't think you will get out of it. What is pure comes to the light. *"He who does the truth comes to the light, that his deeds may be clearly seen, that they have been done in God"* (John 3:21).

The evil power went on to say to this girl, "Go to the railroad station tonight, and there will be a train coming in at 7:32. After you buy a ticket for yourself and your sister, you will have sixpence left. You will find a woman in a railway carriage dressed as a nurse, and opposite her will be a gentleman who has all the money you need." The first thing came true. She bought the tickets and had just sixpence left. Next, the train came in at exactly 7:32. But the next thing did not come true. The two sisters ran from the front to the back of that railroad train before it moved out, and nothing turned out as they had been told. As soon as the train moved out, the same voice came and said, "Over on the other platform." All that night, until 9:30, these two young women were rushed from platform to platform. As soon as it was 9:30, this same evil power said, "Now that I know you will obey me, I will make you the greatest missionaries." It is always something big! They might have known it was all wrong. The evil power said, "This gentleman will take you to a certain bank at a certain corner in Glasgow, where he will deposit all that money for you." Banks are not open at that time of night in Glasgow. If she had gone to the street that this evil spirit mentioned, there probably would not have been a bank there. All they needed was a little common sense, and they would have seen that it was not the Lord. If you have your heart open for this kind of voice, you will soon get into a trap. We must always remember that there are many evil spirits in the world.

Were these sisters delivered? Yes, after terrible travail with God, they were perfectly delivered. Their eyes were opened to see that this thing was not of God but of the Devil. These two sisters are now laboring for the Lord in China and doing a blessed work for Him. If you do get into error along these lines, praise God, there is a way out. I praise God that He will break us down until all pride leaves us. The worst pride we can have is the pride of self-exaltation.

Paul wrote, at the commandment of the Lord,

Let two or three prophets speak, and let the others judge. But if anything is revealed to another who sits by, let the first keep silent. For you can all prophesy one by one, that all may learn and all may be encouraged. (1 Cor. 14:29–31)

If you are not humble enough to allow your prophecy to be judged, it is as surely wrong as you are wrong. Prophecy has to be judged. A meeting such as this one that Paul suggested would certainly be the greatest meeting you ever held. Praise God, the tide will rise to this. It will all come into perfect order when the church is bathed and lost in the great ideal of only glorifying Jesus. Then things will come to pass that will be worthwhile.

Coupled with prophecy, you should see manifested the fruit of the Spirit that is goodness (Gal. 5:22). It was *holy* men who spoke in prophecy in days of old as the Holy Spirit prompted them (2 Pet. 1:21); and so, today, the prophet who can be trusted is a man who is full of goodness, the goodness that is the fruit of the Spirit. But when he gets out of this position and rests on his own individuality, he is in danger of being puffed up and becoming an instrument for the Enemy.

I knew some people who had a wonderful farm; it was very productive and was in a very good neighborhood. They listened to voices telling them to sell everything and go to Africa. These voices had so unhinged them that they had scarcely had time to sell out. They sold their property at a ridiculous price. The same voice told them of a certain ship they were to sail on. When they got to the port, they found there wasn't a ship of that name.

The difficulty was to get them not to believe these false voices. They said perhaps it was the mind of the Lord to give them another ship, and the voice soon gave them the name of another ship. When they reached Africa, they didn't know any language that was spoken there. But the voice did not let them stop. They eventually had to come back brokenhearted, shaken through, and having lost all confidence in everything. If these people had had the sense to go to some men of God who were filled with the Spirit and seek their counsel, they would soon have been persuaded that these voices were not of God. But listening to these voices always brings about a spiritual pride that makes people think that they are superior to their fellow believers, and that they are above taking the counsel of men whom they think are not as filled with the Spirit as they are. If you hear any voices that make you think that you are superior to those whom God has put in the church to rule the church, watch out, for that is surely the Devil.

We read in Revelation 19:10 that *"the testimony of Jesus is the spirit of prophecy."* You will find that true prophetic utterance always exalts the Lamb of God.

FIRE AND FAITH

No prophetic touch is of any use unless there is fire in it. I never expect to be used by God until the fire burns. I feel that if I ever speak, it must be by the Spirit. At the same time, remember that the prophet must prophecy according to the measure of his faith (Rom. 12:6). If you rise up in your weakness, but also in love because you want to honor God, and you just begin, you will find the presence of the Lord upon you. Act in faith, and the Lord will meet you.

May God take us on and on into this glorious fact of faith, so that we may be so in the Holy Spirit that God will work through us along the lines of the miraculous and along the lines of prophecy. When we are

operating in the Spirit, we will always know that it
is no longer we but He who is working through us,
bringing forth what is in His own divine good pleasure (Phil. 2:13).

A True Prophet

The prophet's message is a word of the Lord that has become a burden upon the soul or a fire shut up in the bones—a burden, a pent-up fire, an anguish, and a travail. The word of the Lord is a living flame. The symbol of Pentecost is a tongue of fire.

When the prophet Jeremiah had spoken his message, he felt as if God had let him down and exposed him to ridicule and mockery. He determined to speak no more, but in the silence, the fire burned in his bones. He was full of the fury of the Lord until he was prostrate with holding it in. The fire consumed him until he could no longer hold it in, until one day the fire suddenly leapt forth in forked lightning, or a flaming sword. (See Jeremiah 20:1–11.)

The moment comes when the prophet is full of power by the Spirit of the Lord. He may be called to *"declare to Jacob his transgression and to Israel his sin"* (Micah 3:8). The fire constrains and consumes him, and his generation persecutes and despises his word.

The Lord Jesus came to bring fire (Luke 12:49). He was distressed in spirit, but the baptism that He had to endure was accomplished (v. 50). So it is with every servant of God who brings fire. There is a brooding—a questioning, reasoning, excusing, hoping, foreboding. The whole being is consumed. The very marrow of the bones burns. At first, speech may not, must not, or will not come. Then, in a moment, it suddenly flames out. The prophet becomes a voice through which Another speaks. Fire compels attention; it announces itself. You don't have to advertise a fire. When the fire comes, the multitudes come.

You Have Received—
Now Believe!

God wants to make us pillars: honorable, strong, and holy. God will take us further along in the faith. I am passionately inspired by the great fact of our possibilities in God. God wants you to know that you are saved, cleansed, delivered, and marching on to victory.

"Set your mind on things above" (Col. 3:2); get into the *"heavenly places"* with Christ (Eph. 2:6); *"be transformed by the renewing of your mind"* (Rom. 12:2). What a privilege to kneel and to get right into heaven the moment we pray—where the glory descends, the fire burns, faith is active, and the light dispels the darkness! Mortality hinders, but the life of Jesus eats up mortality. (See 2 Corinthians 5:4.)

MAKE CERTAIN YOU HAVE RECEIVED

The Acts of the Apostles deals with receiving the Holy Spirit, and the Epistles are written to believers

199

baptized in the Holy Spirit. When I was in New Zealand, some brothers in Christ questioned me about this baptism. They quoted the Epistles, but before we are in the experience of the Epistles, we must go through the Acts. I asked them, "When did you speak in mysteries?" (See 1 Corinthians 14:2.) But they had not yet come into the baptism of the Holy Spirit.

JESUS IS GREATER THAN EVERYTHING

Jesus is the life and light of men (John 1:4). No one who has this light walks in darkness. (See 1 John 2:10–11.) *"When Christ who is our life appears, then* [we] *also will appear with Him in glory"* (Col. 3:4). Where His life is, disease cannot remain; where His life is full, deficiencies cannot remain. Is not He who indwells us greater than all? (See 1 John 4:4.) Yes, when He has full control. If we permit one thing into our lives that is outside the will of God, it hinders us in standing against the powers of Satan. We must allow the Word of God to judge us, lest we stand condemned with the world (1 Cor. 11:32). *"When Christ who is our life appears."* Have I any life apart from Him—any joy, any fellowship? Jesus said, *"The ruler of this world is coming, and he has* [finds] *nothing in Me"* (John 14:30). All that is contrary in us is withered by the indwelling life of the Son of God.

THE SPIRIT OF JESUS DWELLS IN US

"We who are in this tent groan, being burdened, not because we want to be unclothed, but further clothed, that mortality may be swallowed up by life" (2 Cor. 5:4). Are we ready; are we clothed? Has mortality

been swallowed up by life? If He who is our life came, we should go with Him. We can live in a heaven on earth right now.

> Heaven has begun with me;
> I am happy, now, and free,
> Since the Comforter has come,
> Since the Comforter has come.

The Comforter is the great Revealer of the kingdom. He came to give us the more abundant life (John 10:10). God has designed the plan. Nothing really matters if the Lord loves us. God sets great store by us. The pure in heart see God (Matt. 5:8). There are no stiff knees, or coughs, or pain, in the Spirit; nothing ails us if we are filled with the Spirit.

> *If the Spirit of Him who raised Jesus from the dead dwells in you, He who raised Christ from the dead will also give life to your mortal bodies through His Spirit who dwells in you.*
> (Rom. 8:11)

THE OVERFLOWING LIFE OF THE SPIRIT

This is what it means to live in the Spirit:

- We are *"free from the law of sin and death"* (Rom. 8:2).
- The *"perfect law of liberty"* (James 1:25) destroys the natural [carnal, sinful] law in us.
- Spiritual activity takes in every passing ray of God's light.
- We live days of heaven on earth.

- We have no sickness, so that we are not aware that we have a body.
- The life of God changes us, bringing us into the heavenly realm, where we reign over principalities and all evil.
- We live a limitless, powerful, supernatural life through the Holy Spirit.

If the natural body decays, the Spirit renews. Spiritual power increases until, with one mind and one heart, the glory is brought down over all the earth, right on into divine life. The whole life is filled as we continue to live in faith.

This is Pentecost! Pentecost means to have the life of the Lord manifested through us wherever we are, whether we are on a bus or a train. We are filled with the life of Jesus unto perfection—rejoicing in *"hope of the glory of God"* (Rom. 5:2) and continually looking for our translation in Christ. The life of the Lord in us draws others as a magnet, and His life eats up everything in us that is not of Him. I must have the overflowing life of the Spirit; God is not pleased with less. It is a disgrace to live an ordinary existence after we are filled with the Holy Spirit. We are to be salt in the earth (Matt. 5:13); we are not to be lukewarm, but hot (Rev. 3:16), which means seeing God with abundance, liberty, movement, and power. Believe! Believe! Amen.

Greater Works:
Experiencing God's Power
Smith Wigglesworth

Smith Wigglesworth was extraordinarily used by God to see souls saved, bodies healed, and lives changed. Even in the face of death, he did not waver in his faith because he trusted the Great Physician. Your heart will be stirred as you read in Wigglesworth's own words the dramatic accounts of miraculous healings of people whom the doctors had given up as hopeless. Discover how God can enable you, too, to reach out to a hurting world and touch all who come your way with His love.

ISBN: 978-0-88368-584-6 • Trade • 576 pages

WHITAKER
HOUSE

Smith Wigglesworth on Healing
Smith Wigglesworth

Meet a bride who is dying of appendicitis, a young man who has been lame for eighteen years, a betrayed husband who is on his way to kill his wife, and a woman who is completely deaf. Through Smith Wigglesworth's words and ministry, you will discover what happened in their lives and what can take place in your own life. Find out how you can personally receive God's healing touch and how God can use you to bring healing to others, just as He did through Smith Wigglesworth.

ISBN: 978-0-88368-426-9 • Trade • 208 pages

WHITAKER
HOUSE

Smith Wigglesworth on Heaven
Smith Wigglesworth

Illustrating his insights with many dramatic, real-life
examples, Smith Wigglesworth has a dynamic message
in store for those who are looking toward the Second
Coming. He explains how to prepare for your future in
eternity with God while experiencing the power and joy
of the Holy Spirit in the present. Discover God's plans
for you in this life and what He has in store for you in
heaven. You can know victorious living—
now and for all eternity.

ISBN: 978-0-88368-954-7 • Trade • 224 pages

WHITAKER
HOUSE

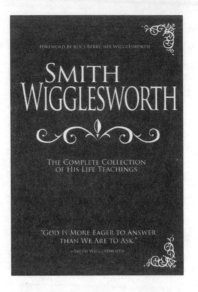

Smith Wigglesworth:
The Complete Collection of His Life Teachings
compiled by Roberts Liardon

Legendary evangelist Smith Wigglesworth dramatically changed the world with his passionate messages. The essence of his dynamic ministry is relived through the complete volume of his life teachings. Sermons have been gathered from archives around the world to create this unequaled treasure. You will see why Smith Wigglesworth is considered the pioneer of the modern Pentecostal faith. Experience the adventure that was Smith Wigglesworth's life. This complete collection of Smith Wigglesworth's powerful sermons is sure to be a classic for countless generations.

ISBN: 978-1-60374-083-8 • Hardcover • 864 pages

WHITAKER
HOUSE

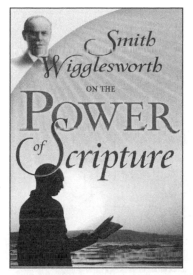

Smith Wigglesworth on the Power of Scripture
compiled by Roberts Liardon

Smith Wigglesworth knew the Bible thoroughly because it was the only book he ever read, and for years, the "Apostle of Faith" exhibited the power of Scripture to millions of believers in his legendary, miracle-filled meetings. Now, many of his teachings have been collected in one book, offering you the rare opportunity to sit at the feet of this anointed man of God. Transcribed exactly as they were delivered to a select group of Bible students, these teachings will allow you to develop your spiritual discernment, claim victory over temptation, and live in the freedom of God's grace. If you are ready to receive a fresh understanding of God's gifts and a fresh anointing of His power, you will cherish this glimpse into the heart and mind of one of His most gifted servants.

ISBN: 978-1-60374-094-4 • Trade • 384 pages

WHITAKER
HOUSE

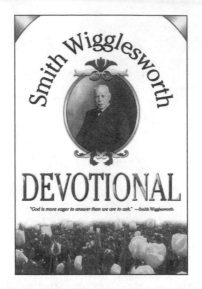

Smith Wigglesworth Devotional
Smith Wigglesworth

You are invited to journey with Smith Wigglesworth on a year-long trip that will quench your spiritual thirst while it radically transforms your faith. As you daily explore these challenging insights from the Apostle of Faith, you will connect with God's glorious power, cast out doubt, and see impossibilities turn into realities. Your prayer life will never be the same again when you personally experience the joy of seeing awesome, powerful results as you extend God's healing grace to others.

ISBN: 978-0-88368-574-7 • Trade • 560 pages

WHITAKER
HOUSE